TELEMENTAL HEALTH with KIDS
Toolbox

Volume 2

125 Competitive Games, Cooperative Play Exercises, Creative Activities, Brain Games, and Talk Therapy Interventions

Amy Marschall, PsyD

Copyright © 2023 by Amy Marschall

Published by
PESI Publishing, Inc.
3839 White Ave
Eau Claire, WI 54703

Cover and Interior Layout: Amy Rubenzer
Editing: Jenessa Jackson, PhD

ISBN: 9781683736240
ISBN: 9781683736257 (ePUB)
ISBN: 9781683736264 (ePDF)

Printed in the United States of America.

PESI Publishing
pesipublishing.com

Dedication

This book is dedicated, once again, to my clients, who inspire me every day.

About the Author

Amy Marschall, PsyD, is a clinical psychologist who has been providing telemental health services since 2017. She is certified in Telehealth and Trauma-Focused Cognitive Behavioral Therapy, and she has been developing and distributing kid-friendly telehealth resources since April 2020. When she is not practicing psychology, she is making art and spending time with her husband and two cats.

Table of Contents

Acknowledgments . . . .**xii**

Introduction . . . .**xv**

Part

1 Competitive Games 1

Animals Minigame Party 2

Badminton 3

Basket Random 4

Bowling 5

Boxing Random 6

Carrom 7

City Car Stunt 8

Dance Party II 9

Darts 10

Donut vs Donut 11

Extreme Thumb War 12

Fish Eat Fishes 13

Food Duel 14

Foosball 3D 15

Get on Top 16

Glowit 17

Gun Mayhem 19

Making Squares 21

Meteor Shower 23

Mini Heads Party 24

Narwhale 25

Othello 26

Parcheesi 27

Penguin Wars 28

Pizza Challenge 29

Polybusiness 30

Pong 31

Pool (8 Ball Billiards Classic) 32

Pop-It 33

Rock, Paper, Scissors 34

Rooftop Snipers 35

Snowball Skirmish 36

Soccer Random 37

Speed 38

Speed Boat Extreme Racing 39

Sprinter Heroes 40

Tube Jumpers 42

Tug-of-War 43

Tug the Table 44

Tunnel Rush 45

Two Ball 3D 46

Volley Random 47

Wrestle Jumping 48

Zilch 49

Part

2 Cooperative Games

Cooperative Games **51**

2048 52

Bad Ice Cream 53

Cuphead 54

Dino Squad Adventure 55

DinoZ City 56

Fireboy and Watergirl 57

Fire of Belief 58

Gun Mayhem Co-Op 59

Interplanetary 60

Ironic Zombie 61

Last Survivors 62

Lost Pyramid 63

Mike & Munk 64

Miners' Adventure 65

Money Movers 66

Space Prison Escape 67

Zombie Mission X 68

Zoom-Be 69

Part

3 Brain Games 71

Beautiful Mind Games 72

Bomb Defuse 74

Bottle Flip. 75

Dadish 76

Find in Mind 77

Find It/Hidden Objects. 78

Hexa Parking 79

Hole 80

Mastermind 82

Pick Up Sticks 84

Riddles 85

Roblox Potion Experiments (Wacky Wizards) 86

Simon. 87

Snowman 88

Tunnel 89

Unfair Mario. 90

Wonderfully Juicy 91

Part

4 Creative Activities 93

Buddha Board. 94

Character Creator 95

Choose Your Own Adventure 97

Color by Numbers 100

Coloring Book 101

Comic Strips. 103

Creating a Sensory Space. 104

Diamond Art 106

Dream Home Design 107

Lite Brite 109

Magnet Poetry 110

Marble Run 111

Plot Generator 112

Timeline 113

Vision Boards: Challenges 115

Vision Boards: Life Goals 117

Vision Boards: What Makes Me Happy? 118

Vision Boards: Who Loves Me? 119

Part
5

Just for Fun 121

Bop It 122

Dress-Up 123

Ducklings 124

Extreme Speedboat Driving 125

Filters 126

Get Over It 127

Good Vibes 128

Nature Cams 129

Paper Airplanes 130

Role-Plays 131

Roller Coaster VR 133

Wish List 135

Part
6

Talk-Based Activities 137

Chat: Secrets 138

Emoji Reactions 139

Mad Libs 140

My Needs 141

My Needs Sample Worksheet 142

Pet Finder 144

Photo Share 145

Projective Cards 147

Story Cards 148

What Would You Do? 149

Part
7

Structured Skill-Building Activities 151

Ads for Mindfulness 152

Breath GIFs 153

Changing the Direction of the Train 154

Daily Behavior Goal 155

Daily Behavior Goal Sample Worksheet. 156

Daily Self-Care Checklist 157

Daily Self-Care Sample Checklist 158

Depression Nesting. 160

Exposure Therapy 162

Five Senses Grounding Technique 163

Press Pause on Impulsivity. 164

Who Would Win?. 166

Part

8 Games by Device 167

Link Share 168

Screen Share with Remote Control 169

Screen Share with Remote Keyboard Control 172

Screen Share (Client). 174

Screen Share without Remote Control. 177

No Tech Available 179

Whiteboards 182

Acknowledgments

Hey, I wrote another book! Here is the part where I get to thank everyone who made this possible. Once again, first and foremost, thank you to everyone at PESI, especially my editors, who walked this journey with me last year and thought it would be a good idea to do it all over again. Special shoutout and thank you to Jenessa Jackson, my editor, and Kate Sample, my contact in the publishing department.

Thank you to my husband and friends, who let me trial run all of these activities before doing them in sessions so I could make sure I had a handle on them before presenting them to clients.

Thank you also to my clients, who trust me with your care, or your child's care. I truly have the greatest job in the world.

Introduction

In 2020, child therapists scrambled to transfer their practices online as a result of the COVID-19 pandemic—forcing them to figure out how to provide virtual interventions that kept kids engaged but still provided evidence-based outcomes. In response, I created the first volume of the *Telemental Health with Kids Toolbox*, which provided detailed instructions for setting up a telehealth practice and included more than 100 ready-made, kid-friendly activities. Since that time, telehealth services have continued to grow, which has opened the door for more accessible care to kids living in rural areas, families with transportation issues, and immunocompromised clients. The silver lining of the pandemic has been that we have increased accessibility, and these changes are here to stay.

If you read my first *Telehealth and Kids Toolbox*, you gained access to a wealth of telehealth-friendly therapeutic activities for your child and teen clients. This sequel has two goals: to more than double the size of your intervention toolbox and to organize the interventions into an easy-to-use directory based on what resources you have available in a given session. When it comes to working with kids, you can never have too many interventions at your disposal. Maybe your clients have tried many of your existing games and activities and would like to try something new. Maybe you want to take new approaches to treating different diagnoses or challenges. Or maybe you just want a greater repertoire of interventions that are tailored to each client's unique interests, treatment goals, and developmental level. Whatever your reason for wanting to incorporate a larger range of activities into your telehealth practice, you can find over 125 additional options and solutions here.

As an added benefit, this book also includes a directory of activities from *both* volumes that sorts interventions based on the telehealth features available to a given client. For example, are you meeting with a client from school where wireless restrictions are in place? Is your client unable to access remote screen control? I have broken down the available activities based on these limitations to make it easier than ever to figure out what resources you have at your disposal in a given session. In this directory, you'll find:

- Activities that work when the child is connected to Wi-Fi that blocks most game websites
- Activities that work if you are unable to use the screen share function
- Activities for smaller screens such as smartphones
- Activities that require the client to have access to a keyboard

For most of the activities in this book, I have included links to specific websites that I use in my telehealth sessions. If a link is not working for you, I recommend putting the name of the activity into a search engine. Most of these games are sourced in multiple places, and you should be able to find most of the games on other platforms. Like the first volume, I have included suggested age ranges, therapeutic benefits, and specific instructions for each of these interventions.

As you sort through the variety of activities and therapeutic games in this toolbox, use your clinical judgment to determine which activities are the best fit for each client. Explore which activities from the first toolbox were most successful for you. What did your clients respond to, and what did they enjoy about those activities? Use that information as a starting point when deciding which interventions to try first. Above all, remember to be flexible and have fun!

1

Competitive Games

Competitive games are a central part of play therapy. You can observe how a client handles winning and losing, how they respond to rules and boundaries, and what happens when they get frustrated. You can also use competitive games as an opportunity to practice emotion regulation and coping skills in real time when the game does not go the child's way. Many times, I have noticed a child making progress in their ability to self-regulate when they lose a game and say, "Good game!" instead of "You cheated!" It also goes without saying that many kids also like competitive games because it gives them an opportunity to "beat" the therapist.

In this section, you will find 44 competitive games for use in your telehealth sessions. Each involves games with specific rules and a clearly defined winner and loser. Some of these activities require the use of multiple keys to navigate the game, while others are simpler one-click games that involve pressing only one key, which you can use with clients as young as four years old. I find the one-click games helpful when you are trying to talk through something that happened in the child's life. These games free up just enough space in their brain that they tend to feel more comfortable talking to you.

Animals Minigame Party

Suggested Age Group: 6 and up

Therapeutic Benefits: Teamwork, emotion regulation, decision-making, focus

Telehealth Benefits: This activity includes fun animal animations and several simple games to choose from. The activities are easy to master and great for building rapport. You can work together or play competitively, depending on what skills you want to focus on.

Setup: Go to https://www.crazygames.com/game/animals-minigame-party and share your screen. Grant your client remote control so they can control their character. The game will prompt you to choose four animal avatars, allowing you to play with up to four humans. If you are using this activity for a one-on-one session, you and your client will each pick an animal, and the other two animals will be controlled by the computer (AI). You can choose a difficulty level for the AI avatars between easy, normal, or hard. The human-controlled avatars move using the W, A, S, and D keys; the arrow keys; the I, J, K, and L keys; and the T, F, G, and H keys. The game shows you which controls each avatar uses.

Once you have selected avatars, you can choose from several minigames. Games include Ball Dodge (played like dodgeball), Star Catch, and Ball Kick. Some games are player versus player, and others use teams of two. If you choose a two-player game, you and your client can choose to be on the same team and work together.

Badminton

Suggested Age Group: 8 and up

Therapeutic Benefits: Focus, impulse control, frustration tolerance, emotion regulation

Telehealth Benefits: The in-person version of badminton can be challenging for you to incorporate in session, as most do not have access to a badminton court, and the physical nature of the game can interfere with talk-based interventions. In addition, physical games can be inaccessible for clients and therapists with mobility issues. This telehealth version of badminton keeps your client engaged and allows you to connect with them throughout the session while sidestepping all these concerns.

Setup: Go to https://www.twoplayergames.org/game/stick-badminton-2, select *2 Player*, share your screen, and grant your client remote control. Each player gets to choose what character they want to be. Personally, my favorite option is the toaster.

Player 1 is controlled by the W (jump), A (move), S (swing), and D (move) keys, and Player 2 is controlled with the arrows (right and left for move, up to jump, and down to swing). The controls are simple, but the game is particularly difficult to master because of the way the characters and the birdie move, as well as how carefully you need to time your shots in order to successfully return the serve. This can bring up opportunities to de-escalate and practice regulation skills as you play the game. Sometimes kids want to "rage quit" this activity, but if you can encourage them to try to finish at least one full game, you can get a lot of great skill practice in.

Basket Random

Suggested Age Group: 6 and up

Therapeutic Benefits: Focus, rapport building, frustration tolerance

Telehealth Benefits: This quick basketball activity helps hold your client's attention on the device and the session, while also having simple enough controls that you can talk during the game. Learning to play is easy and the games are quick, so you can play several times in a row. The scene changes frequently, which makes this game great for holding attention in kids with focus issues such as ADHD.

Setup: Go to https://www.twoplayergames.org/game/basket-random, select *2P*, share your screen, and grant your client remote control. Both you and your client each control two basketball players. One person controls their team with the W key, while the other person controls them with the up arrow. You can control whether players jump forward or backward by tapping the control key when they are leaning one way or the other. The goal is to score the most baskets.

Therapy Tip: Whoever scores a basket gets to ask a question of the other person. This builds rapport and helps the child feel comfortable in their session.

Bowling

Suggested Age Group: 4 and up

Therapeutic Benefits: Focus, frustration tolerance, taking turns, boundary work

Telehealth Benefits: I have a small foam bowling set in my in-person office, which kids absolutely love. The trouble I run into is that offices are typically not large enough for people to easily bowl, and pins like to roll too far out of reach. That's one of the benefits of doing a telehealth version of this activity! It also imposes rules and structure that allow you to do boundary work without sacrificing rapport. Another benefit of the telehealth version is that it keeps score for you so you don't have to tally it yourself (and it prevents cheating). When kids are losing and can't change their score, I find opportunities to sit with their frustration and cope with dissatisfaction.

Setup: Go to https://www.crazygames.com/game/3d-bowling and select the two-player option. You can choose to play a full 10-frame game or a faster 5-frame game, depending on the length of your session, your client's attention span, and what other interventions you might want to save time for. Grant your client remote control of your screen so you can take turns, and decide who will go first.

You control the ball by clicking and dragging. When it is your turn, bowl! This game follows standard bowling rules: You get two tries to knock down as many of the 10 pins as you can. Take turns and see who can get the most points.

Therapy Tip: If you would like, you can prompt your client to share a feeling, something they like, or something related to one of their treatment goals for every pin they miss (or for every pin they knock down).

Boxing Random

Suggested Age Group: 6 and up

Therapeutic Benefits: Focus, rapport building, frustration tolerance, aggression work

Telehealth Benefits: As with Basket Random, this game is simple and easy to learn. However, Boxing Random is even more basic in that each player has only one character, so it is great for clients who struggle with executive functioning issues. This makes it easier to engage clients and hold their attention while you work through emotions in real time or implement a talk intervention. The activity also has an aggressive component, so it is well suited to aggression work and anger processing.

Setup: Go to https://www.twoplayergames.org/game/boxing-random, select *2P*, share your screen, and grant your client remote control. One player uses the W key to move, while the other uses the up arrow. The object of the game is to punch the other player before they punch you. Whoever scores five rounds first wins the game.

Therapy Tip: As your client plays the game, prompt them to visualize the source of their anger. Have them imagine they are punching that anger source. Once the game is over, see how this visualization impacts how they are feeling, and then work together to process that feeling.

Carrom

Suggested Age Group: 7 and up

Therapeutic Benefits: Emotion regulation, frustration tolerance, rapport building, taking turns

Telehealth Benefits: You save time playing this game online because you do not have to physically set up the pieces. In addition, the game room has rules coded in, so if you or your client are unsure about the rules of the game, you can learn as you go by just playing.

Rules: Carrom, also known as Karom, is a Southeast Asian game played on a square board with nine black pieces, nine white pieces, and one red piece called the Queen. The Queen is in the very center, with the black and white pieces surrounding it in two circles, with all pieces touching. Each player has a slider that they use to try to knock their pieces into one of four pockets (one in each corner), similar to a game of pool.

Players sit across from each other and take turns trying to knock their pieces into the pockets. The player who goes first tries to pocket the white pieces, and the player who goes second tries to pocket the black pieces. Players also try to pocket the Queen but must "cover" this piece by pocketing one of their own pieces right after pocketing the Queen. If the Queen is not "covered," it is placed back in the center of the board.

At the start of your turn, the slider is placed on your side of the board, and you attempt to strike your pieces. If you pocket one of your pieces on your turn, you get to go again until you miss. There are specific rules regarding how to touch your slider, though this is not relevant when playing online. The game ends after the Queen is covered and one player has pocketed all nine of their pieces. You want to be the first player to pocket all of their pieces.

Setup: Go to https://www.crazygames.com/game/carrom-online, click *tap to start*, and select *private game*. Then choose a password; usually something simple and easy to communicate to your client is appropriate, like their first name or 123. The game will provide a link, which you can copy and send to your client via your telehealth platform's chat feature. When they follow the link, they will join you in the room. The person who creates the room goes first, so if you want to give your client the option to go first, you can talk them through setting up the room.

Therapy Tip: You can choose to simply play the game for relationship building or real-time emotion regulation work, or you can allow whoever pockets a piece to ask the other a question about a memory, coping skill, or emotion.

City Car Stunt

Suggested Age Group: 6 and up

Therapeutic Benefits: Planning and strategy, focus, executive functioning, emotion regulation

Telehealth Benefits: In my in-person office, many kids enjoy playing with matchbox cars and having us race them. This activity brings that interest into the telehealth session with a more exciting and structured version of racing. Though the client cannot design their own track, if your goal is to work on emotion regulation and practice planning skills that come from the racing itself, the telehealth version saves time and adds boundaries to the activity.

Setup: Go to https://www.twoplayergames.org/game/city-car-stunt-4, share your screen, and grant your client remote control. You can choose the free driving option if you just want to practice with the controls or have fun with this activity. However, for a competitive game with a bit more structure, choose the racing option and select *2 Player*. The first player selects their car, followed by the second player. When you have both chosen your cars, click *next*.

There are several levels and different tracks available in this game, though you have to play and unlock each of them. You might want to play this game on your own for a while before using it in a session, as this will allow you to get more comfortable with playing the game, or you can unlock the levels together with a client.

Player 1 appears on the left and uses the arrow keys to control the car. Player 2 is on the right and uses the W, A, S, and D keys to control the car. Then, you race! As you race, the game will offer statistics about your speed, acceleration, brake power, and steering.

Dance Party II

Suggested Age Group: 8 and up

Therapeutic Benefits: Focus, fine motor skills, frustration tolerance, patience

Telehealth Benefits: Many kids enjoy incorporating music and dance into their sessions. If you want to engage kids with this interest while participating in competitive play, Dance Party II is a great resource. Although full-body work is important, this activity only requires finger-based movement, leading to lower risk for injury for kids with motor skills deficits.

Setup: You can access this game at https://kizi.com/games/super-Friday-night-funki or https://arcadespot.com/game/super-Friday-night-funkin/. Pull up the game on your web browser and share your screen. Various levels with indicated difficulty will appear. You have to unlock levels before they are all available, so you might want to take some time to play this game on your own to make all levels available before you use this in sessions.

Like the video game *Dance Dance Revolution*, this online game plays music as different steps scroll across the screen. You use the arrow keys to follow the steps, pressing the corresponding key when both arrows line up at the top of the screen. You and your client take turns on each level using screen control to see who can achieve a higher score.

Since this game involves taking turns, your client has to practice patience when you complete your run. The game is based on skill, and you can vary the difficulty level based on your client's preference and needs. As clients work to improve their skill, you can help them practice coping skills for anger and frustration in real time.

Darts

Suggested Age Group: 5 and up

Therapeutic Benefits: Focus, executive functioning, frustration tolerance, emotion regulation

Telehealth Benefits: Darts can be a lot of fun but are not always a safe option for in-person sessions, making it well-suited for telehealth. This activity tests your client's ability to focus and promotes emotion regulation skills in a fun way.

Setup: Go to https://www.coolmathgames.com/0-darts and select *human versus human*, choose a nickname (or have the computer generate a random nickname), and select *okay*. To start a new game, click on *create match* and enter a password. I recommend using a password to ensure that your client is the only one who can join your game room. Then click *create*.

Once you are done creating the room, send your client the same generic link to the website using your platform's chat feature. Instruct them to join the room that corresponds with your nickname. When the game loads, they will also choose *human versus human*, select a nickname, and press *okay*. They will see the match you created listed under "join a match." Have them click on your match to join. When your client enters the game room, the match will start automatically.

When the match starts, you will see the dart board in front of you, with an animated dart moving slowly across the screen. Aim the dart by clicking when it is in the position from which you want to throw it. Then click and drag with your mouse to determine how hard and at what angle you will throw your dart. The game has you take turns playing and keeps score for each round.

At the end of the round, the game prompts you to do the math to total your own score. Some clients find this annoying, but it can help them regulate their emotions if they are feeling frustrated with the game, as it distracts them and gives them a chance to de-escalate. If you tally your score incorrectly, the number of darts on your next turn reduces by one, which becomes an opportunity to practice a frustration coping skill in the session.

Therapy Tip: To help your client explore their emotions further, ask them to assign an emotion to each color on the dart board (black, beige, red, and green) and have them give an example of a time they felt that emotion each time the dart lands on that color. You can also assign different thoughts or behaviors to each color instead. If you play the game this way, you can have clients skip their turn if they get a bull's-eye.

Donut vs Donut

Suggested Age Group: 6 and up

Therapeutic Benefits: Impulse control, emotion regulation, planning and strategy, following rules, social skills, aggression work

Telehealth Benefits: This is a great activity that involves aggressive play, making telehealth an ideal setting where kids can act out these impulses in a physically safe way. It also has cute animations of donuts, and it goes without saying that most kids like donuts!

Setup: Go to https://www.crazygames.com/game/donut-vs-donut, share your screen, and grant your client remote control. Then choose the number of players you want (for an individual session, select *2P*). You and your client will each choose what color donut you want to be. Each donut is controlled by a different letter: green is Q, blue is P, orange is M, and pink is C. If you are playing with just one client, the other two donuts will be controlled by AI (artificial intelligence). The goal of the game is to push the other three donuts out of the circle so you are the last donut standing. The game is very simple, and you control your donut by pressing the control key.

Because you and your client will both have access to a full keyboard to play this game, it is possible for you or your client to cheat by trying to control each other's donuts. You will have to trust each other not to do this, and it will require your client to use their impulse control skills. This makes Donut vs Donut one of the few competitive telehealth games where it is possible to break the rules coded into the game. It is a great option for clients who are working on learning to play fairly.

Extreme Thumb War

Suggested Age Group: 6 and up

Therapeutic Benefits: Focus, frustration tolerance, boundaries, impulse control

Telehealth Benefits: Most people are familiar with the concept of a thumb war. With the telehealth setting, you eliminate the risk that you or your client will accidentally get hurt while playing. The game also definitively declares a winner of each round and has set time limits, so you can practice enforcing boundaries without impacting rapport.

Setup: Go to https://www.twoplayergames.org/game/extreme-thumb-war, share your screen, and grant your client remote control. Choose *2 Player*, and decide which thumb is yours and which is your client's. When the game starts, you click on your thumb, and your client clicks on theirs. The goal is to hit your client's thumb while it is down and to simultaneously avoid having your thumb hit while it is down. The game is best out of three, so you must win two rounds to win. The graphics are not bloody or disturbing, but the activity has an aggressive component, which allows clients to safely work through angry emotions in real time.

Fish Eat Fishes

Suggested Age Group: 5 and up

Therapeutic Benefits: Focus, emotion regulation, coping skills, anger management

Telehealth Benefits: This is a fun, quick game that can serve as an analogy for the issues your client is struggling with outside of your sessions. The cute, animated characters draw young kids in, and each round is pretty short, so this works even for those with short attention spans.

Setup: This game can be played with one, two, or three players. Go to https://www.crazygames.com/game/fish-eat-fishes, share your screen, and grant your client remote access. Select the number of players and click the arrows to choose what fish you each want to be. If you are doing a two-player game, Player 1 is controlled with the W, A, S, and D keys, and Player 2 is controlled with the arrow keys. When the game starts, various predators appear on the screen and attempt to eat you. The goal is to be the last player standing. Use your control keys to dodge them for as long as you can.

Therapy Tip: For an added therapeutic component, you can tell your client to imagine that the various predators on the screen represent triggers for their trauma, anger, or problem behaviors. Label each predator with a corresponding trigger and practice dodging them. You can then discuss coping skills and resources that your client can use to dodge these triggers in real life.

Food Duel

Suggested Age Group: 4 and up

Therapeutic Benefits: Impulse control, focus, emotion regulation, anger management

Telehealth Benefits: This game requires players to respond to specific stimuli and to ignore others, making it great for impulse control work. If you are familiar with the card game Slap Jack, it draws on similar skills without requiring players to hit each other, making this telehealth activity safer and more therapeutically appropriate. Kids love the cute, animated animals too.

Setup: Go to https://www.crazygames.com/game/funny-food-duel, select *2 Player*, share your screen, and grant your client remote control. You and your client each get to pick which pet you want to be in the game. After you have each chosen your player, click the crossed swords in the middle to start the game. Player 1 is controlled with the A key, and Player 2 is controlled with the left arrow. The game presents you with various food that is either rotten, frozen, or good to eat. Your goal is to eat the good food before your opponent but not to eat frozen or rotten food. The first player to get eight points wins, but you lose a point each time you eat something you are not supposed to.

Therapy Tip: Think of the food as things your client "consumes" in their life. What things allow them to gain "points" (make them feel good and help them be the best version of themselves)? What things "freeze" them (get in the way of a good choice, like watching online videos instead of doing homework)? And what things make them "sick" (trigger problem behaviors)?

Foosball 3D

Suggested Age Group: 6 and up

Therapeutic Benefits: Focus, frustration tolerance, exploration of emotions

Telehealth Benefits: Foosball is an activity that a lot of kids have fun with, but it is not typically feasible to keep a foosball table in a therapy office due to how much space it takes up. With telehealth, you can have as many virtual game boards and machines as you want. You also do not risk losing the ball or breaking the table because your client got angry and kicked it.

Setup: Go to https://www.crazygames.com/game/foosball-3d, share your screen, and grant your client remote control. Decide which team each of you will be on. The player with the goal on the left side of the screen uses W and S to move the rods back and forth, and A and D to kick. The player with the goal on the right side uses the up and down arrows to move the rods, and the left and right arrows to kick. You are trying to score more goals than your opponent to win the game.

This is an expansion of a previous telehealth version of foosball that was previously available. The 3D option is more complicated, as there are additional controls, so it is a great option for kids who want to be more challenged by the game.

Therapy Tip: If you would like, make a list of feelings with your client before starting the game. Whenever someone either scores a goal (or the other team scores a goal on them), they choose an emotion and share a time they felt that way, or they can demonstrate what that emotion looks like on their face.

Get on Top

Suggested Age Group: 6 and up

Therapeutic Benefits: Focus, frustration tolerance, planning and strategy

Telehealth Benefits: This is a virtual wrestling activity, so it's a great way to work on aggressive impulses without risking injury to yourself or your client. Since the program decides the winner, you can also maintain boundaries and rules without sacrificing rapport.

Setup: Go to https://www.twoplayergames.org/game/get-on-top, select *2P*, share your screen, and grant your client remote control. Decide who will be the first player and who will be second player. The first player uses the W, A, S, and D keys to move, and the second player uses the arrow keys.

Each player tries to pin the other by getting on top using their control keys. When you pin your opponent, their head comes off, and you win that round. If you slip up, it is difficult to recover. In my experience, once one player has an edge, they have a very high chance of winning the round. This can be frustrating because your client does not have the opportunity to recover, but they can always try again!

The game is quick and can be played several times in a session. You can keep score to determine an ultimate champion or simply play multiple times.

Therapy Tip: One great thing about quick games like this is that your client can learn that they can still win even if they lost in previous rounds. They can learn from their mistakes, instead of letting these mistakes define them, and try to improve over time.

Glowit

Suggested Age Group: 5 and up

Therapeutic Benefits: Taking turns, frustration tolerance, emotion regulation, listening

Telehealth Benefits: If you ever have an indecisive client who says, "I don't know" when you allow them to choose an activity for their session, Glowit is a great option. It is actually 12 games in one, and you don't get to choose which game to play because it randomly chooses for you when you click play. This can also help kids who struggle with following directions because they have to practice doing an activity they did not choose. It can also help kids who have trouble making decisions because it takes the pressure off of them (though that is only appropriate if you are not currently working on enhancing decision-making skills). All activities have simple controls and rules that are easy to learn.

Setup: Go to https://www.crazygames.com/game/glowit-two-players, share your screen, and click the arrow in the middle of the screen. All games allow you and your client to take turns, so you can alternate remote control on the screen. At the start of each activity, it lets you know what color each player is and walks you through the instructions. After each round, you can replay that game or randomly choose another game. Glowit keeps score across several games, so if you want to keep track of who wins the most games, you easily can. Each round is less than five minutes long, so this activity can be engaging for kids who have trouble with focus and attention.

The mini games within Glowit are:

1. **Basketball:** Take turns trying to score baskets. The first to score three baskets wins.

2. **Cars:** You take turns "shooting" your car down a road that contains various obstacles. Whoever crosses the finish line first wins the round.

3. **Target Shooting:** Try to knock all of your opponent's targets off of the board before they knock all of yours off of the board.

4. **Soccer:** Each person has multiple players and takes turns attempting to kick the soccer ball into the other players' goal. You try to score the most points.

5. **Mini Pool:** Take turns trying to knock balls into pockets. The first person to knock three balls into pockets wins.

6. **Break Blocks:** Go through three rounds of aiming a ball at blocks, and see who can hit the most blocks over the course of three turns.

7. **Cats:** You and your client take turns trying to fling cats on top of a pedestal. The winner is whoever has the most cats on the pedestal at the end of the round.

8. **Can Ball:** Over three rounds, try to knock more cans off of a pedestal than your opponent.

9. **Bottle Flip:** Take turns flipping bottles onto a platform. Whoever lands the most bottles on the platforms wins the round.

10. **Ice Cube Shooting:** Try to land more ice cubes in the glass than your opponent.

11. **Shoot the Balls:** You start with three balls on each side, and you take turns trying to shoot the balls through a moving opening in the wall. The winner is whoever is able to get all the balls on the other side first.

12. **Tower Fall:** Take turns breaking a block on a tower, and try not to make the tower fall, similar to Jenga.

Gun Mayhem

Suggested Age Group: 10 and up

Therapeutic Benefits: Frustration tolerance, planning and strategy, regulating aggression

Telehealth Benefits: Some kids have an interest in weapons and aggressive play, and this is a safe way to work through aggression without risk to you or your client. Since I encourage clients to bring activities that interest them to sessions, they sometimes suggest shooting games that are extremely graphic and might not be appropriate. The animations in this game are simple and not gruesome, so this can be a good compromise in engaging this interest without exposing the client to graphic content.

Setup: Go to https://www.twoplayergames.org/game/gun-mayhem, select *custom game*, and choose which of the five available games you and your client want to do. Share your screen and grant your client screen control so you can each control your character. The five game options are:

1. **Last Man Standing:** The last player standing wins the game. You can decide how many lives you have at the start of the game and choose whether weapons are dropped from the sky in crates or generated on the ground.

2. **Last Man Standing (Team Mode):** This mode is the same as Last Man Standing but uses teams. This could be used for group therapy, or you can have AI players join you. If you use AI, you can either team up with your client or have AIs help each of you. This mode does not require that the teams be evenly matched, so you can allow your client to have an advantage in the game.

3. **Duck Survival:** The goal for Duck Survival is to survive for as long as you can while AIs try to kill you. You and your client see who can stay alive the longest.

4. **Gun Game:** In this version, you and your client have unlimited lives. You are trying to upgrade your weapons, and the winner gets and uses all the weapons and upgrades first. This version is popular among kids who have an interest in weaponry.

5. **1 Hit 1 Kill:** You and your client are each given only five shots per life. You have to use your ammunition carefully to win.

Once you have chosen what version of the game you want to play, you and your client can customize your characters if desired. You can choose a hat, shirt, gun, and player color. Each player can also choose whether or not they want to have a specific perk, like faster speed, no gun recoil, extra ammunition, or extra grenades. Player 1 uses the arrow keys to move, [to shoot, and] to use bombs. Player 2 uses the W, A, S, and D keys to move, T to shoot, and Y to use bombs. You can use the settings feature to customize controls if you would prefer.

If your client enjoys this activity but gets bored with this specific version, you can also play Gun Mayhem 2 More Mayhem (https://www.twoplayergames.org/game/gun-mayhem-2-more-mayhem) and Gun Mayhem Redux (https://www.twoplayergames.org/game/gun-mayhem-redux).

Making Squares

Suggested Age Group: 6 and up

Therapeutic Benefits: Planning and strategy, taking turns, frustration tolerance

Telehealth Benefits: This classic dot and box game is one that you can also use for in-person sessions, but the virtual format allows you to play without acquiring any supplies. Since the activity simply involves connecting dots to create squares, you can easily engage in talk therapy while playing, and the activity can distract your client from their anxiety about exploring emotions without pulling them out of the conversation altogether. At the same time, the activity itself fosters various skills, such as strategizing and taking turns, and can be a therapeutic tool on its own.

Setup: You can create your own dot grid or simply do an image search for "dot graph paper." The next page contains an example that you can scan and use in your sessions. Pull up the image, share your screen, and prompt your client to open the annotate function in their telehealth platform. Each of you chooses a color so that you remember who made each line.

Decide who will go first. When it is your turn, draw either a horizontal or vertical line between two dots. The goal of this activity is to have the highest number of squares when there are no spaces left for new lines. If your line completes a square, you get another turn. Fill in the square with your color so you know it is yours.

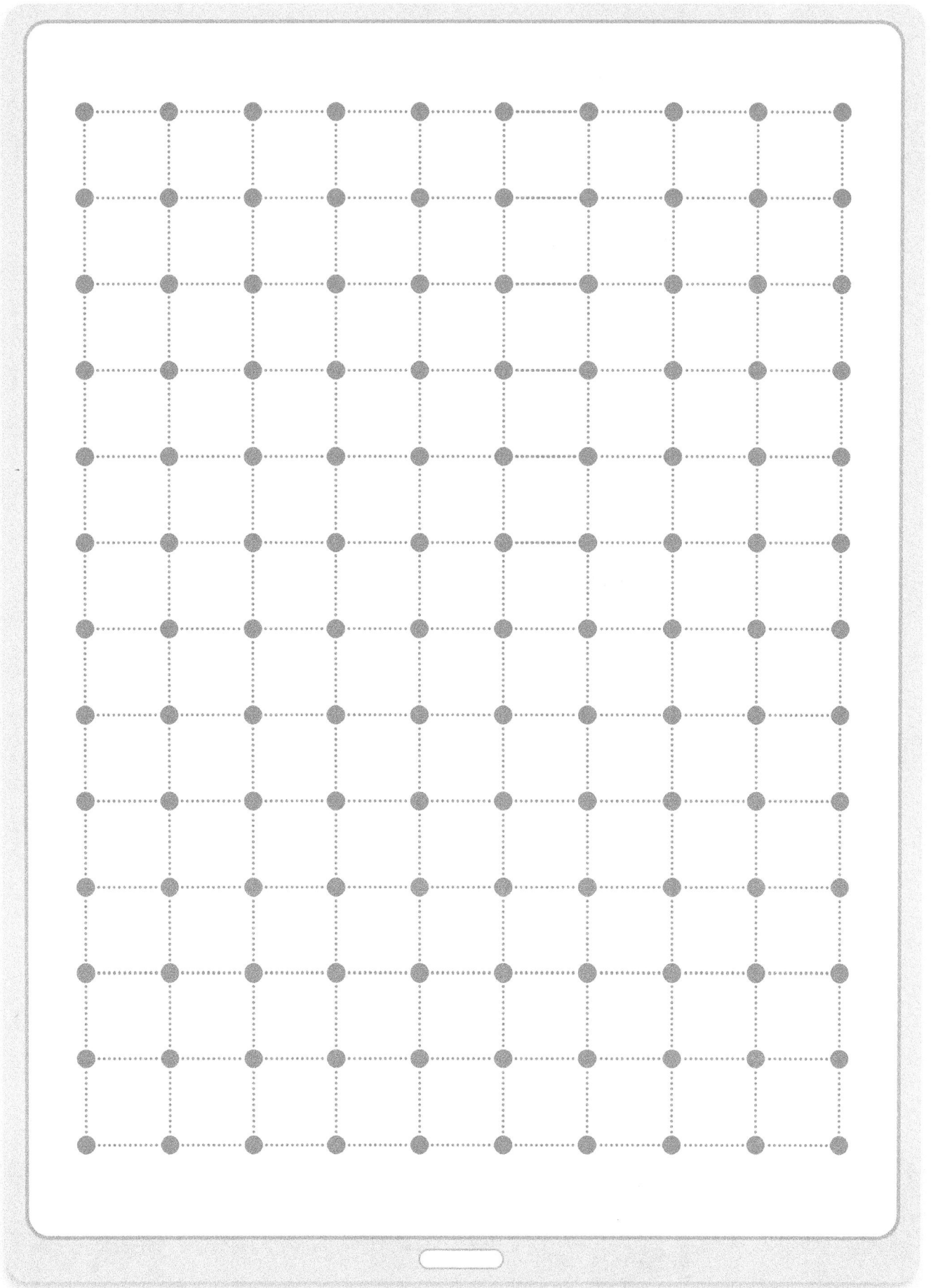

Meteor Shower

Suggested Age Group: 5 and up

Therapeutic Benefits: Focus, frustration tolerance, exploration of emotions

Telehealth Benefits: This is a game that does not have an in-person option. I really like finding telehealth activities like this because it demonstrates that not only is telehealth a viable alternative to in-person sessions, but it also has its own offerings that would not otherwise be possible. This is a fun and simple game that kids can easily learn and play.

Setup: Go to https://www.crazygames.com/game/meteor-shower and choose *2 player mode*. Share your screen and grant your client remote control access to the game.

The object of the game is to survive longer than the other player. When the game starts, meteors begin to cross the screen. Each player is a small circle that bounces around the screen. This game is controlled with one key, with Player 1 using the space bar and Player 2 using the zero key (0). The key makes your player change direction, which you can do to dodge the meteors. Whoever goes the longest without getting struck by a meteor is the winner! This is usually a quick game, so you can play it several times to see if you can last longer than the time before.

Therapy Tip: After each game, use the following therapeutic prompts that either the winner or loser has to answer:

1. Talk about a time you felt [emotion].

2. What is something you wish you could do better?

3. What is something you are proud of?

4. What is a mistake you have made?

5. What is something you wish you would have known a year ago?

6. What is something you hope is different about your life in a year?

7. What is the best compliment you have ever gotten?

8. How do you handle challenges?

9. How do you know when you need to ask for help?

10. What is the strangest dream you have ever had?

Mini Heads Party

Suggested Age Group: 8 and up

Therapeutic Benefits: Decision-making, frustration tolerance, emotion regulation, shifting

Telehealth Benefits: This activity provides several games to choose from, which allows your client to practice making a decision, but there is also the option to have the computer randomly select a game. Different activities pull different focus and problem-solving skills, and the quick changes in the activity help keep the game novel and interesting for clients with attention issues.

Setup: Go to https://www.twoplayergames.org/game/mini-heads-party, choose *2 players*, and click *OK*. You and your client can each choose what color you want to be in the game. Once you have decided who is Player 1 and who is Player 2, and have both selected your colors, click *OK* to start the game. Player 1 can move using either the W, A, S, and D keys or the Z, Q, S, and D keys. Player 2 moves with arrows or with the I, J, K, and L keys. There are five activities to choose from:

1. The first game is soccer, and the first to score five goals wins. There is a weapon on the field, and whoever picks it up gets the advantage of being able to shoot at the other player.

2. The second game involves trying to get the most chickens in your pen. As with the soccer game, there is a weapon on the field that you can use to shoot at your opponent if you are able to pick it up first.

3. In the third game, you and your opponent are chased by ghosts. Whoever survives the longest wins.

4. Both players are preparing food for customers, and whoever prepares the most food in the time frame wins.

5. Both players try to avoid being eaten by a monster, and the winner is whoever survives the longest.

Let your client choose a game (or, if they are struggling to decide, choose a game that is developmentally appropriate for them). After each round, you choose a new game, so this activity involves transitions and ongoing decision-making.

Narwhale

Suggested Age Group: 6 and up

Therapeutic Benefits: Planning and strategy, frustration tolerance, motor skills, aggression work

Telehealth Benefits: Narwhale is a fun and engaging activity that allows kids to act out aggressive impulses in a safe environment and requires them to manage frustration and setbacks in real time. The animations are simple and cute, and kids get excited to pretend to be a narwhal.

Setup: Share this link with your client: http://narwhale.io/. When you load the page, the website will ask you to input a name. You can type any username into the text box, and you do not have to create an account to play. From the dropdown menu, you can choose rooms based on size (large, sparse, small) or activity. Activities include Narwhale Ball (soccer), Narwhale Egg Hunt (teams try to get the most Easter eggs into their goal), and Death Match (players are eliminated one at a time until only one remains). Each room name has parentheses after it that show the number of players presently in the room. Decide with your client which room you will enter.

You might choose a room that has other players in it or a room that is empty. If you choose a room with several players, you can try to play cooperatively and protect each other. However, in an empty room, you and your client can play against each other. In Narwhale Ball and Narwhale Egg Hunt, you are randomly assigned a team when you join, so if you want to make sure you and your client are not on the same team, you will want to choose an empty room. Since the game does not have a chat feature, the presence of other players does not forfeit confidentiality and privacy.

Once in the room, you control your narwhal with your mouse. Click to make the narwhal lunge and stab. The object of the game is to survive, and you level up by attacking other players. When you attack someone, you cut them in half. If you are cut in half, you have to start over and lose any benefits you earned from leveling up. Some of the rooms include other activities, such as trying to get a ball into another player's goal or collecting Easter eggs for points.

Othello

Suggested Age Group: 6 and up

Therapeutic Benefits: Planning and strategy, focus, executive functioning, problem-solving

Telehealth Benefits: As with all telehealth board games, the online version of Othello eliminates the need for cleanup, and you will never lose pieces again. The game also keeps score for you, so you can keep track of who is winning without taking focus off of the conversation.

Setup: The game is available at many websites, including https://www.eothello.com/. This website shows you what moves you have to choose from at the start of each turn, which can make it easier for your client to learn the rules. One player chooses to be the white pieces, and the other is the black pieces. The game starts with four pieces in the middle of the board (two white and two black—both websites listed above start the game off with this setup). The player with the black pieces goes first.

When it is your turn, you place a piece on the board. The piece must be placed adjacent to one of your opponent's pieces in such a way that there is a line from your piece across the opponent's piece(s) to another of your pieces. Any of your opponent's pieces that become captured in between your pieces are then "flipped" to your color. If your move creates more than one line, you get to flip all lines of your opponent's pieces as long as one of your pieces was already at the end of that line. The game ends when the board is full, and the winner is whoever has the most pieces on the board at this time.

Parcheesi

Suggested Age Group: 6 and up

Therapeutic Benefits: Taking turns, frustration tolerance, exploration of emotions, safety planning, boundaries

Telehealth Benefits: As with all board games, telehealth prevents you from ever losing pieces, and games never experience damage or wear and tear. The telehealth version of this game allows you to enforce rules and boundaries without sacrificing rapport.

Setup: Go to https://www.crazygames.com/game/parcheesi, choose *human versus human mode*, and select the disc colors for each player. Share your screen, and take turns by alternating screen control with your client. The game can be played with two to four players. Parcheesi is a board game similar to Sorry, Trouble, and Ludo.

To play, you roll two dice on each turn. (You roll the dice by clicking on the icon with your disc color.) If you roll a 5 or two dice equaling 5, you can move a piece out of your "nest." Once a piece is out of your nest, your goal is to move it to the home space. The number of spaces you can move is determined by your dice roll. For example, if you roll a 3 + 6, you can move your piece nine spaces—or if you have two pieces on the board, you can move one piece three spaces and another piece six spaces. If you roll doubles, you can make four moves: one for each number on top of the die and one for each number on the bottom of the die. If you roll doubles, you also get to roll again.

There are safe spaces around the board. You cannot land on a safe space if an opponent's piece is on that space. Two pieces from the same player can be on a space at the same time, and when this occurs, it forms a blockade, and the opponent cannot pass that space. Landing on a space occupied by the opponent that is not a safe space sends the opponent's piece back to their nest. You win the game by getting all four of your pieces into the home space first.

Therapy Tip: Because the board contains safe spaces where your opponent cannot get you, and there is a safety zone before you reach your home square, this activity offers an additional opportunity to talk to your client about safety. You can also use the blockades as a way to talk about setting boundaries, maintaining boundaries, and respecting boundaries set by others.

Penguin Wars

Suggested Age Group: 5 and up

Therapeutic Benefits: Taking turns, problem-solving, logic, frustration tolerance, emotion regulation, aggression work, decision-making

Telehealth Benefits: This game lets kids explore aggressive play without any overt violent images or risk to themselves or to you. Plus, who doesn't love penguins?

Setup: Go to https://www.crazygames.com/game/penguin-wars, select *2 player game*, share your screen, and take turns with remote control. In this game, you and your client each play three animated penguins who are trying to knock the other three penguins off of their iceberg. When it is your turn, drag your mouse to adjust the angle and force of your throw, and then click *fire* to see if you can hit the opponent's penguins. The first person to knock all three penguins down wins the round.

You can choose between a snowball, grenade, and rocket to fire at the other side. Choose carefully, though—you can throw unlimited snowballs but can only use one grenade and one rocket per game. If you do not get the angle right and miss, you will not get another chance to use it.

If you choose to play in New Campaign mode, you and your client can unlock different scenes and play multiple settings. You'll want to play through on your own first if you want to unlock all levels and let your client choose which one they want to play.

Therapy Tip: At the start of the round, assign each penguin an emotion. When that penguin gets knocked over, share a time when you felt that way. Similarly, you can make the rule that whoever knocks a penguin down gets to ask the other person one question.

Pizza Challenge

Suggested Age Group: 6 and up

Therapeutic Benefits: Frustration tolerance, emotion regulation, motor skills, focus

Telehealth Benefits: This is a quick and fun activity that engages your client and builds rapport. It is a quick game, so you can play once or several times, depending on your client's attention span. Each round has a winner and loser, and you have the option to tally how many times each of you wins, but you do not have to do this, so you can decide how competitive you want the activity to be.

Setup: Go to https://www.twoplayergames.org/game/pizza-challenge, choose *2P*, share your screen, and grant your client remote control. One player uses the W key, and the other uses the up arrow. The object of this activity is to grab the most slices of pizza off of the tray—it is as simple as that! Time your grabs to get as many slices as you can, and try to get more slices than the other player.

Polybusiness

Suggested Age Group: 8 and up

Therapeutic Benefits: Problem-solving, frustration tolerance, planning and strategy, decision-making, executive functioning

Telehealth Benefits: Polybusiness is essentially off-brand *Monopoly*. In my experience, it can be difficult to play Monopoly in an in-person therapy session because the game has so many components to keep track of that you can easily lose focus of the therapeutic side of the activity. With the telehealth version, the computer automatically tracks all transitions, how much money you have, and which properties you own, allowing you to focus on your client's emotional response to the activity or a side discussion. In addition, the computer-coded rules prevent cheating and allows your client to sit with feelings of frustration when the game does not go the way they want it to go, rather than allowing them to change the rules to avoid this discomfort.

Setup: Go to https://www.crazygames.com/game/polybusiness and share your screen. When the game loads, click on *add local player* two times (or more if you are doing this activity with a group). You cannot choose each player's color, but you can allow your client to decide what color they want to be from the options generated. Once you are ready to play, alternate remote control with your client. Since turns for this game are entirely point-and-click, you can also play this game if your client is unable to control your screen from their device. Instead, your client can simply tell you what choices to make when it is their turn.

The game starts with instructions, detailing that you take turns rolling, purchase unclaimed properties that you land on, and earn money by passing Go or having your opponent land on one of your properties. The object of the game is to not run out of money.

As with traditional *Monopoly*, this game can take a long time. Unfortunately, the Polybusiness website does not allow you to save progress, so you might not be able to finish a game in a session and cannot pick up where you left off in the last session. However, this can be helpful for clients who struggle with losing, as the unfinished game technically has no winner or loser.

Pong

Suggested Age Group: 6 and up

Therapeutic Benefits: Motor skills, focus, executive functioning, emotion regulation, trauma processing

Telehealth Benefits: I find games like Pong helpful when first processing trauma memories with my clients because they can decide how deeply to focus on the memory versus the game. This allows them to have some control over how intensely they reexperience what happened to them, which can help them become more comfortable with engaging. And unlike the in-person version this game, you don't have to worry about purchasing a ping-pong table or damaging things in your office.

Setup: Go to https://pong-2.com/, select *multiplayer*, share your screen, and grant your client remote control. The player on the left uses the W and S keys to control their paddle, and the player on the right uses the up and down arrows. The goal of the game is to outscore your opponent. The game continues until one person reaches 10 points.

Variation: For a similar game with a more challenging layout, you can play Pinball Clash, which has the feel of Pong but the obstacles of classic Pinball. Go to https://www.crazygames.com/game/pinball-clash, choose *keyboard controls*, and select *switch AI* in the lower-left corner to create a two-player game. Share your screen and grant your client remote control. The player on the left controls their flippers with the A and Z keys, and the player on the right controls theirs with the K and M keys. Kids who enjoy pinball but want a more challenging or varied game may appreciate this variation.

Therapy Tip: To get your client talking more about their emotions, you can choose a prompt for when they score, such as "Name a feeling you experienced this week."

Pool (8 Ball Billiards Classic)

Suggested Age Group: 8 and up

Therapeutic Benefits: Motor skills, mindfulness, emotion regulation, patience, taking turns

Telehealth Benefits: 8 Ball Billiards Classic can be a very mindful activity that draws on a lot of skills, but most therapy offices do not have the space to feasibly offer it as an activity. Once again, telehealth comes to the rescue by offering a virtual space that does not take up any room. Most clients have some familiarity with this game, and the rules are simple and easy to learn.

Setup: Many websites offer two-player pool games, and you can search and try different ones to see what features are the best fit for you. I prefer this classic version: https://www.crazygames.com/game/8-ball-billiards-classic. Pull up the website, select *human versus human*, and share your screen. You and your client will take turns with screen control to take your shots. To take a shot, move your cursor to the desired position, hold down your mouse while dragging the pool stick backward, and then let go. Whoever lands a ball in a pocket first is that team (stripes or solids). When you land a shot, you get another turn. If you miss, the turn passes. Once you get all of your balls in pockets, you must land the 8 ball. You have to call where the 8 ball will land; if the 8 ball lands in a different pocket, you lose.

If you are doing therapy with a group, you can also play this activity with two teams, with each player rotating through their turn as a stripe or solid.

Pop-It

Suggested Age Group: 6 and up

Therapeutic Benefits: Planning and strategy, taking turns, frustration tolerance

Telehealth Benefits: The fidgets that I use for my in-person sessions have a shelf life—they wear out over time from so many kids playing with them. Virtual fidgets like this one never break or wear out. If something glitches, you can always refresh the screen and start over!

Setup: There are many virtual pop-it games available online. One that works well for this activity is https://www.crazygames.com/game/pop-it-3d. Load the game, make sure all of the pokable bubbles are facing the same way, and share your screen. You can simply use this as a virtual fidget for your client to use during the session, or you can make a simple game out of it.

To turn it into a game, alternate remote-control access and take turns popping bubbles. When it is your turn, you can pop any number of bubbles in one row, as long as they are in the same row. You can start your turn on a row that already has some bubbles popped or on a row that has not yet been touched. Your goal is to make your opponent pop the last bubble on the pop-it. This game is easy to learn and incorporates an item that many kids enjoy and might not have access to at home.

Rock, Paper, Scissors

Suggested Age Group: 4 and up

Therapeutic Benefits: Planning and strategy, frustration tolerance, focus

Telehealth Benefits: When you play this game face to face, you sometimes begin to notice "tells" in the other person that help you predict what they are going to throw. In the telehealth version, however, you do not see your opponent's hand, which makes it more difficult to predict what the other player will choose. The game also keeps score for you, so you do not have to track it yourself.

Setup: Go to https://www.twoplayergames.org/game/roshambo and select *2P*. Share your screen and grant your client remote control. Decide who will be orange and who will be blue. The orange hand is controlled with the A (rock), S (paper), and D (scissors) keys, and the blue hand is controlled with the J (scissors), K (paper), and L (rock) keys. You press the letter that corresponds with your choice each round.

Therapy Tip: You can simply use this fun activity to build rapport or have the winner or loser share something about themselves after each round. For example, you can have the winner say something they like about themselves or ask the loser to share something that worries them.

Rooftop Snipers

Suggested Age Group: 10 and up

Therapeutic Benefits: Planning and strategy, impulse control, executive functioning, emotion regulation, focus, aggression work

Telehealth Benefits: Many kids like to incorporate aggressive themes into their play, and while Nerf guns can be a safe way to explore this, they can be inappropriate or unsafe in a small office space. Some therapists are also uncomfortable having weapon toys in their office. This telehealth alternative provides a safe and fun way to incorporate aggression work into a session.

Setup: Go to https://www.crazygames.com/game/rooftop-snipers, click the arrow in the center of the screen, and choose the two player option. Share your screen and grant your client remote control. One player is red, and the other is blue. The red player jumps with the W key and shoots with the E key, and the blue player jumps with the I key and shoots with the O key. Press and hold your shooting key to aim at the other person. The objective of the game is to make your opponent fall off of the roof first by shooting them. You have to be careful, though—if you jump too many times and lose your balance, you can fall and cost yourself the round.

With each round, the background changes and different obstacles show up. For example, on one level, there are boxes between you and your opponent, and you have to jump over them or shoot them out of the way to get to your opponent. The weapons also change; in one level, you throw axes at each other instead of shooting guns.

Therapy Tip: For an added therapeutic component, whoever falls off the roof first can share a memory of a time when they did something challenging.

Snowball Skirmish

Suggested Age Group: 5 and up

Therapeutic Benefits: Emotion regulation, frustration tolerance, planning and strategy

Telehealth Benefits: Snowball fights are exciting and a lot of fun, but they are not practical for a therapy session. Depending on the time of year and where you live, the weather makes this impossible. In addition, the safety and confidentiality logistics of an in-person snowball fight are prohibitive. But within the telehealth setting, you and your client can safely throw things at each other.

Setup: Go to https://www.crazygames.com/game/snowball-skirmish, share your screen, and grant your client remote control. There are three different maps you can choose from for your snowball fight, though they are all similar. You can play multiple times on different maps. The goal is to hit the other player with your snowballs while dodging their snowballs. Player 1 jumps with the W key, moves with the A and D keys, and throws snowballs using the space bar. Player 2 uses the arrow keys to jump and move, and throws snowballs using the L key. You each get five lives, and whoever lasts the longest is the winner. After a round ends, you can restart the game on the same map or return to the main menu to choose another map.

Therapy Tip: Whoever wins a round can share something they are good at or something they like about themselves.

Soccer Random

Suggested Age Group: 6 and up

Therapeutic Benefits: Focus, rapport building, frustration tolerance

Telehealth Benefits: This game is very similar to Basket Random, but with soccer instead of basketball. The setup and rules are the same, but having options lets you tap into different clients' interests. With the continuous changes to the scenery and one-key instructions, you and your client can learn the game quickly while still holding your attention with novel stimuli.

Setup: Go to https://www.twoplayergames.org/game/soccer-random, select *2P*, share your screen, and grant your client remote control. One player uses the W key to control their team, while the other uses the up arrow. When one of your team members comes into contact with the ball, they kick it toward the other goal. Whoever scores five goals first wins.

Therapy Tip: For a self-esteem intervention, have each player say something they are good at or something they like about themselves whenever they score a goal.

Speed

Suggested Age Group: 8 and up

Therapeutic Benefits: Planning and strategy, frustration tolerance, emotion regulation

Telehealth Benefits: This game involves fast decision-making, and by playing virtually, you can avoid accidentally hitting or injuring each other. The virtual option also enforces the game's rules, setting boundaries with your client without you having to do so, which could interfere with the relationship.

Setup: Go to https://www.crazygames.com/game/speed-the-card-game, log in as a guest, and click *online* to create a private room. There are two ways to create a private room, both of which require you and your client to pull up the website in a web browser. For the first method, you can choose *play a friend*, which automatically generates an invite code you can send your client to join the room. For the second method, you can choose *private room*, and you and your client input the same room name. The room names must match exactly. An easy way to do this is to use your name or your client's name.

Each player starts with a hand of five cards and a draw pile from which they can draw cards if they are unable to play at any point. Two cards are placed face up in the center (called the play pile), with pull piles next to each of them. Using your mouse, quickly place cards that are one value above or below one of the center cards. For example, a 10 can be placed on a jack or a 9. As the name suggests, the objective is to do this as fast as you can so you can outpace your opponent.

If you cannot play and have fewer than five cards in your hand, draw cards from your draw pile until you have a total of five again. If neither player can play any cards and both players have five cards in their hands, flip new center cards from the pull piles. You win by playing all the cards in your deck first.

Speed Boat Extreme Racing

Suggested Age Group: 6 and up

Therapeutic Benefits: Focus, executive functioning, emotion regulation, decision-making

Telehealth Benefits: This racing game is perfect for kids who have an interest in boats, as it increases their engagement with the intervention. It also brings a level of excitement that is not always possible with in-person activities, which can help kids learn to regulate in real time.

Setup: Go to https://www.twoplayergames.org/game/speed-boat-extreme-racing, select *race mode*, and select *2P mode*. Share your screen and grant your client remote control. You will each choose which boat you want to drive and which track you want to race on. Player 1 uses the W, A, S, and D keys to steer, while Player 2 uses the arrow keys. Follow the track to complete the race. You and your client will also race against various AIs for an extra challenge.

There is also a free drive mode that you can use to practice controlling the boats, going over jumps, and steering before engaging in the racing activity. You can use free drive mode for a non-directive take on this game as well.

Sprinter Heroes

Suggested Age Group: 7 and up

Therapeutic Benefits: Impulse control, frustration tolerance, focus

Telehealth Benefits: Racing games can be difficult to incorporate into in-person sessions due to space issues, making them ideal for telehealth. Games that are only feasible in a virtual format can draw in clients who are apprehensive about starting telehealth, as it makes the telehealth session feel special.

Setup: Go to https://www.crazygames.com/game/sprinter-game, choose *2P*, share your screen, and grant your client remote control. You can each choose your player from several options. Once you have both made your choices, click the arrow on the screen to begin. There are several continents to choose from, but they need to be unlocked. You can either work together to unlock all the continents or play on your own before a session and let your client choose where they want the race to take place.

Player 1 runs using the A and D keys, and Player 2 uses the left and right arrows. You must alternate between the two keys or your character will trip, costing you time. Your goal is to win the race, which is between the two of you and six AI runners. Between you, your client, and the AIs, you can place anywhere from first to eighth place. You accumulate points based on what place you each take, so you can play several tracks and choose an overall winner if desired.

Therapy Tip: Choose eight questions to represent first through eighth place, and have your client answer based on how they place in each round. Although choosing questions together can be a fun activity as well, suggested questions can include:

1. If you could magically change one thing about your life, what would you change?

2. What movie or TV show do you relate to and why?

3. What is a dream you had recently that you remember?

4. If you could meet one famous person, who would you meet, and what would you say to them?

5. What makes someone your best friend?

6. What is something that you wish the people in charge understood about you?

7. What is something you do that you would like to take a break from?

8. What is something you need help doing?

Tube Jumpers

Suggested Age Group: 5 and up

Therapeutic Benefits: Frustration tolerance, emotion regulation, focus

Telehealth Benefits: This is a quick and easy game that uses a single key command, making it well-suited for young kids. The added option of being able to play with a larger group is great for family work as well.

Setup: Go to https://www.crazygames.com/game/tube-jumpers. This game can be played with two, three, or four players, so you can use it for a family session or small group if you would like. For individual sessions, select *2 players*. Each player enters their name (you can use nicknames if you prefer) and chooses what color they want to be.

This game uses single key control: Player 1 uses W, Player 2 uses I, Player 3 uses Z, and Player 4 uses M. Each player presses their command key to indicate that they are ready to start the game. Once the game begins, each player begins riding their tube, which is being pulled behind a boat. As the boat hits waves and bumps, players need to try to stay in their tubes. Whoever stays in the tube longest wins.

Therapy Tip: Whoever falls out of the tube first shares a time that they struggled.

Tug-of-War

Suggested Age Group: 6 and up

Therapeutic Benefits: Focus, rapport building, emotion regulation

Telehealth Benefits: Tug-of-war can be a fun competitive activity, but it is hard to play this game safely in person. In addition, given their size, adult therapists have an unfair advantage over most child clients. This online version levels the playing field and allows you to play the game safely.

Setup: Go to https://www.twoplayergames.org/game/tug-war, select *2P*, share your screen, and grant your client remote control. Player 1 uses the W key to pull the rope, while Player 2 uses the up arrow. The goal of the game is to pull the other player over to your side of the screen. The first person to score five rounds wins the game. Although the game keeps score, the scoring sometimes glitches. This creates an opportunity to talk about fairness and manage disappointment.

Therapy Tip: Before the game, choose a big feeling that your client often experiences. At the end of each round, have whoever won that round share a coping skill that helps them manage that feeling.

Tug the Table

Suggested Age Group: 6 and up

Therapeutic Benefits: Focus, rapport building, frustration tolerance

Telehealth Benefits: This game is similar to Basket Random, Soccer Random, Tug-of-War, and Boxing Random in that it is played with one key control that is easy to master. This makes it easy to hold your client's attention while still leaving room to implement talk-based interventions or work through frustration and emotion regulation in real time.

Setup: Go to https://www.twoplayergames.org/game/tug-the-table, select *2P*, share your screen, and grant your client remote control. One player uses the W key to pull their end of the table, while the other player uses the up arrow. The goal is to pull the other player across the line in the center of the screen. The game also randomly generates explosives. The first person to score five rounds wins the game.

Therapy Tip: Whenever someone wins a round, have them share an achievement they worked hard for. It can be an award of some kind, a skill they mastered with sustained effort, or a time they solved a problem.

Tunnel Rush

Suggested Age Group: 6 and up

Therapeutic Benefits: Focus, impulse control, frustration tolerance, emotion regulation

Telehealth Benefits: This is a fast-paced game that is a lot of fun for kids. It requires them to stay attuned to the activity and regulate their emotions to master the game. Most in-person therapy games do not have this level of action as you play, so this game can be more engaging than most traditional therapy games.

Setup: Go to https://poki.com/en/g/tunnel-rush and choose *2 Player*. Decide who will be the left and right sides of the screen (left is controlled with the W, A, S, and D keys, and right is controlled with the arrow keys). This activity has the feel of a racing game, though both players move at the same speed. As you move through the tunnel, barriers will come up. Use your command keys to tilt back and forth so you can dodge these barriers. Whoever is able to get farthest in the tunnel without hitting a barrier wins the round! The game can easily be reset, and you can play as many times as you want.

Two Ball 3D

Suggested Age Group: 6 and up

Therapeutic Benefits: Focus, impulse control, frustration tolerance, executive functioning

Telehealth Benefits: This activity has similarities to Tunnel Rush, but the graphics are brighter, and there is the added goal of collecting diamonds as you play (which can be incentivizing!). Kids really enjoy the graphics and movement, and if they play repeatedly, they can see themselves get better in real time.

Setup: Go to https://www.twoplayergames.org/game/two-ball-3d, share your screen, and grant your client remote control. Decide who will be the ball on the left and who will be the ball on the right. The left ball is controlled with the W, A, S, and D keys, and the ball on the right is controlled with the arrow keys. Once you have decided who will be playing each ball, select *2P Play* to begin.

The game has two objectives: to stay on track longer than your opponent and to collect diamonds. Each round ends when someone falls off of the track. Diamonds can be used to upgrade your ball to make the game easier.

Volley Random

Suggested Age Group: 6 and up

Therapeutic Benefits: Focus, rapport building, emotion regulation

Telehealth Benefits: This activity is similar to Basket Random and Soccer Random in that it is quick, easy, and holds your client's attention while leaving room for conversation and talk-based interventions during the game.

Setup: Go to https://www.twoplayergames.org/game/volley-random, select *2P*, share your screen, and grant your client remote control. One player controls their team with the W key, while the other controls them with the up arrow. You aim your characters by having them jump when they are leaning forward or backward. The goal is to hit the volleyball back and forth until your team scores. The first team to score five rounds wins the game.

Therapy Tip: Have whoever wins each round share a conflict they have experienced, either one they overcame or one they are still struggling with.

Wrestle Jumping

Suggested Age Group: 6 and up

Therapeutic Benefits: Focus, rapport building, anger work

Telehealth Benefits: Like Boxing Random, this is an aggressive, one-key game that lets clients act out anger or aggressive impulses in the safe telehealth environment.

Setup: Go to https://www.twoplayergames.org/game/wrestle-jumping, select *2P*, share your screen, and grant your client remote control. This game involves two wrestlers, one of whom is controlled by the W key, and the other by the up arrow. The goal of the game is to pin your opponent down by hitting their head on the ground. The first person to beat their opponent five times wins.

Therapy Tip: After each round, have your client practice making faces of different emotions on their camera. Encourage them to make exaggerated faces to express their feelings as big as they can.

Zilch

Suggested Age Group: 6 and up

Therapeutic Benefits: Focus, executive functioning, planning and strategy, taking turns

Telehealth Benefits: This activity can work for either individual or group therapy because you can have as many players as you want. Keeping score can be a bit challenging, but this pulls clients in and keeps them engaged in the session. In the telehealth version, you also do not have to worry about losing dice, which is a nice perk. Because it is a game of luck and strategy, it also taps into children's executive functioning skills without making them feel like they are "working" on these skills.

Setup: You can play Zilch in a telehealth session if you and your client each have six dice at home. If this is not an option, you can use virtual dice rollers at https://www.calculator .net/dice-roller.html or https://www.random.org/dice/. You can share your screen and alternate remote control to roll the six dice. You will need either paper and pen or an electronic spreadsheet to keep score. If you use a spreadsheet, you can code it to add up scores for you.

In Zilch, players take turns rolling six dice to accumulate points. You must accumulate at least 500 points before you can start scoring and get on the board. On subsequent turns, you only need to accumulate 350 points before you begin scoring. Dice are scored as follows:

- 5s are 50 points each

- 1s are 100 points each

- Three of a kind equals that number times 100 (so three 2s are 200 points, three 3s are 300 points, etc.), but three 1s are 1,000 points

- A straight (1, 2, 3, 4, 5, 6) is 1,500 points

- Any three pairs are 2,000 points (for example: 2, 2, 4, 4, 6, 6)

- Any two triplets are 3,000 points (for example: 3, 3, 3, 4, 4, 4)

- Any four of a kind is 4,000 points

- Any five of a kind is 5,000 points

- Any six of a kind is 6,000 points

After you roll, pull any scoring dice and put them to the side. You can re-roll any dice that were not put aside or re-roll all the dice if they were all put aside (for example, if you roll a straight, you re-roll all six dice). You can continue rolling as long as you continue to accumulate points, and your turn is over either when you "bank" (when you choose to stop rolling and save the points you have collected during your turn) or when you roll a Zilch (a roll that is not worth any points). A Zilch roll means you accumulate zero points for that turn.

If you have the minimum score to bank your points, you can pass your turn to the next player. However, if you roll your remaining dice and do not score, you get Zilch and lose all points for that turn. To win the game, you must be the first to surpass the winning number of points. Some versions of the game have this cutoff at 15,000 points, and others have it at 10,000. You can choose a higher number if desired.

2

Cooperative Games

Cooperative games have similar therapeutic benefits to competitive games—they rely on a specific structure and set of rules, and they often require problem-solving and strategizing in order to win—but unlike competitive games, they require you and your client to work together. These games are a great way to build rapport because you are joining forces against a common enemy, and the only way to win is through teamwork. In addition to reinforcing prosocial behaviors, cooperative play also emphasizes other important social skills, such as asking for help and effective communication.

Kids with anger issues or aggression can get a lot of benefit from cooperative play, as it puts them in a position where they succeed from working together rather than trying to beat you or win. This section contains 18 cooperative games for use in your telehealth sessions, though some activities described in the competitive games section can also be used for cooperative play if you set them up in such a way that you and your client are playing on the same team. The games in this section focus specifically on activities that require you and your client to work together to achieve a common goal or objective.

2048

Suggested Age Group: 6 and up

Therapeutic Benefits: Communication skills, teamwork, social skills, planning and strategy

Telehealth Benefits: To my knowledge, there is not an in-person version of this game (unless you and your client use a tablet or laptop during your in-person session). This fun and relatively simple game requires you and your client to work together to overcome a challenge.

Setup: Go to http://www.reenigne.org/2p2048/, share your screen, and grant your client remote control. One of you will use the arrow keys, and the other will use the mouse. If your client is using a tablet or smartphone for their session, it is easiest if they are the mouse player and you are the keyboard player.

Your goal is to create a block that is worth 2048 without filling the grid and getting stuck. When it is the keyboard player's turn, they press an arrow key to move all blocks on the board in a chosen direction. When it is the mouse player's turn, they left click to place a 2 block or right click to place a 4 block. You must move the blocks each turn in order to continue the game.

In the original 2048 game, new blocks are generated randomly, but in this version, the mouse player decides where they will appear. You and your client need to communicate with each other and strategize about where to place various blocks and in what direction to move them to ensure that you win the game.

Bad Ice Cream

Suggested Age Group: 6 and up

Therapeutic Benefits: Communication skills, planning and strategy, teamwork, frustration tolerance, emotion regulation

Telehealth Benefits: It is a well-known fact that most kids like ice cream. In this cooperative action-arcade game, you and your client are both ice cream cones trying to collect all the fruit without getting squished by enemies! What a fun and creative way to work together toward a common goal. As you play, the levels increase in difficulty, requiring real-time emotion regulation and de-escalation skills.

Setup: There are three versions of this game available at the time of this writing:

1. **Bad Ice Cream:** https://badicecreamgame.com/

2. **Bad Ice Cream 2:** https://badicecreamgame.com/bad-ice-cream-2

3. **Bad Ice Cream 3:** https://badicecreamgame.com/bad-ice-cream-3

Each version has more tricks and twists than the one before, and levels get more difficult as you play. You can choose which version and level to present to your client based on their developmental level, skills, and comfort with the game. You can present increasing difficulty over time to show your client that they can learn to master challenges and show them how they have improved over time.

Once you decide which version of the game to play, share your screen and grant remote control to your client. You each choose what flavor of ice cream you want to be from vanilla, chocolate, and strawberry (later versions of the game have even more flavor options). One player uses the W, A, S, and D keys to move and the F key to make or destroy ice blocks, and the other player uses the arrow keys to move and the space bar to make and destroy ice blocks.

Each level has different fruits that you and your client need to collect, but there are also enemies that you must avoid. Different enemies act differently, with some moving faster than others, some following a specific pattern, some following your avatar around the screen, and some able to break through the ice blocks. If an enemy touches you, you are squished! You can have the other player try to complete the level or start over, depending on how you prefer to play.

Cuphead

Suggested Age Group: 7 and up

Therapeutic Benefits: Communication skills, focus, emotion regulation, strategy, problem-solving

Telehealth Benefits: If a client is a fan of traditional video games, they're likely familiar with Cuphead, a two-player video game that is known for being challenging and difficult to beat. But you don't need a gaming system to play it in your telehealth sessions! The online version is just as challenging and requires a lot of focus, while allowing you to work together to defeat a common enemy. Although the controls are easy to learn, the game itself is difficult to master and has varying difficulty levels, allowing you to use the same activity in increasingly challenging ways.

Setup: Go to https://www.crazygames.com/game/cuphead, share your screen, and grant remote control to your client. You can choose your difficulty level from simple, regular, expert, and invisible challenge. I suggest starting with simple, especially if you have never played before. Again, this game has a reputation for being challenging.

Choose if you want to play with the arrow keys; the W, A, S, and D keys; or custom keys. Custom keys give your client the option to decide what they controls they want to use in the game. If you play using the arrow keys, the controls are: Z to parry, X to shoot, C to shrink, V to use the EX move (a powered-up, special attack that deals a lot of damage), and Q to switch weapons. With the W, A, S, D keys, the controls are: F to parry, space bar to shoot, E to shrink, R to use the EX move, and Q to switch weapons. The game prompts you with these controls at the start in case you forget.

To play Cuphead as a cooperative game, decide which of you will control the character's movement and which will control the weapons. In my experience, clients like to be in charge of shooting the boss, but giving them the option can help with engagement and buy-in. The goal is to destroy the boss before the boss destroys you and to survive the level. You get three lives, so if you do not dodge every single attack, you can still win the game. However, once you lose a life, you cannot get it back, so be careful!

Dino Squad Adventure

Suggested Age Group: 6 and up

Therapeutic Benefits: Teamwork, communication skills, planning and strategy, frustration tolerance, imagination

Telehealth Benefits: This is a great activity for kids who like dinosaurs. It is also good for cooperative play, but since many of the levels include dodging or fighting enemies, you can bond over a common enemy. This is particularly helpful for kids who have a hard time with cooperative play because they have a strong need to win in games. Since this is an online game, the enemies move randomly, so it requires more focus and strategy than traditional cooperative board games.

Setup: Go to https://www.crazygames.com/game/dino-squad-adventure, share your screen, and grant your client remote control so you can both play simultaneously. There are multiple levels you can choose from, though they have to be unlocked before you can play them. You have the option to unlock levels alongside your client or unlock them by playing on your own and then allow your client to decide which level they want to play.

One dinosaur is controlled with the W, A, S, and D keys, and the other is controlled with the arrow keys. Decide who will be playing each dinosaur before starting the game. The dinosaur controlled by the arrow keys can jump while holding onto the wall, allowing it to climb to places the other cannot reach, while the dinosaur controlled with the W, A, S, and D keys can fire a gun with the F key. This dinosaur is the only one who has a gun.

The dinosaurs have to work together using these skills to collect all the coins, which can be a great starting point for talking about different strengths and times that we might need to ask for help. After you have collected all the coins on the level, you must run to the castle. Each dinosaur gets three lives, so you can make a mistake or get hurt and the level does not have to start over as long as you have other lives remaining. If either of you is killed, you have to restart the level.

If your client enjoys this activity but has finished all the levels, they can also play Dino Squad Adventure 2 at https://www.twoplayergames.org/game/dino-squad-adventure-2 and Dino Squad Adventure 3 at https://www.twoplayergames.org/game/dino-squad-adventure-3.

DinoZ City

Suggested Age Group: 8 and up

Therapeutic Benefits: Teamwork, communication skills, frustration tolerance, executive functioning, imagination, aggression work

Telehealth Benefits: So many kids love playing with dinosaurs and shooting at things, but sometimes these activities can get a bit aggressive or overstimulating during in-person sessions. DinoZ City translates these activities into a telehealth format, allowing you and your client to work together to save people from dinosaurs! I wish they allowed you to customize the characters, but there are some fun features that this game has to offer.

Setup: Go to https://www.twoplayergames.org/game/dinoz-city, share your screen, and grant your client remote control. Choose the two-player option and decide who will be Player 1 and Player 2. There are multiple levels you can choose from, though they have to be unlocked before you can play them. You can play the game on your own and unlock the levels prior to using the game in your sessions, or you can work with your client to unlock them together. Some kids enjoy knowing that they helped you unlock each level.

Player 1 uses the following control keys: W, A, S, and D to move, F to fire their weapon, H to throw a grenade, and Q to switch weapons. Player 1 can also slide on a wall using W. Player 2 uses the following control keys: arrows to move, L to fire their weapon, J to throw a grenade, and U to switch weapons. The up arrow also allows Player 2 to slide on the wall.

Your goal is to save the humans from escaped dinosaurs, collect dinosaur eggs, take down the dinosaurs, and stay safe while doing so. Each player gets three hearts (or lives), and you can heal by eating cheeseburgers that you pick up along the way. You can upgrade to more powerful weapons by collecting them as you go. As you rescue people, some help you—for example, by shooting at dinosaurs after you heal them. This is a great way for kids to work out aggression cooperatively while engaging with their interests. The levels also get progressively more challenging.

Fireboy and Watergirl

Suggested Age Group: 8 and up

Therapeutic Benefits: Teamwork, communication skills, strengths work, problem-solving

Telehealth Benefits: This activity offers another great way to engage cooperatively with your client to overcome challenges. In this game, the focus is on gathering diamonds rather than fighting enemies, so this is a great option for kids who are not working on aggressive impulses or who prefer not to engage in aggressive play.

Setup: There are several versions of this game. Below are the various Fireboy and Watergirl games:

1. **Forest Temple:** https://www.crazygames.com/game/fireboy-and-watergirl-the-forest-temple

2. **Light Temple:** https://www.coolmathgames.com/0-fireboy-watergirl-2-light-temple

3. **Ice Temple:** https://www.coolmathgames.com/0-fireboy-watergirl-3-ice-temple

4. **Crystal Temple:** https://www.coolmathgames.com/0-fireboy-watergirl-4-crystal-temple

5. **Elements:** https://www.coolmathgames.com/0-fireboy-watergirl-5-elements

You can play these activities over telehealth by sharing your screen and granting your client remote control. Fireboy is controlled with the arrow keys, and Watergirl is controlled with the W, A, and D keys. The two characters work together to solve various puzzles and levels. Fireboy can walk through lava but is destroyed by water, and Watergirl is dried up in lava but can walk through water. You must also collect diamonds, some of which a specific character has to reach. As with many of these cooperative games, you and your client have to help each other using each character's strengths to survive and accomplish tasks.

Therapy Tip: Fire and water are opposites, and the characters in this game are destroyed by opposite things. This opens up the opportunity to discuss how a quality can be either a strength or a deficit depending on how it is used or the context in which it is presented.

Fire of Belief

Suggested Age Group: 12 and up

Therapeutic Benefits: Teamwork, communication skills, exploration of emotions, problem-solving, frustration tolerance

Telehealth Benefits: This game is particularly engaging for adolescent clients who are not excited at the prospect of talk therapy. The game has a darker aesthetic that can draw in clients who feel like their interests are "dark" or "weird" compared to their peers, or those who identify with emo or goth identities. Additionally, it combines teamwork and problem-solving in a fun and unique way.

Setup: Go to https://www.crazygames.com/game/the-fire-of-belief, share your screen, and grant screen control to play this with a client. Player 1 uses the W, A, S, and D keys to move, while Player 2 uses the arrow keys. The two players work together to solve a series of puzzles by finding clues in various levels of the game. The home screen gives you the option to view truths, which you unlock as you play through. You can play this using a standard QWERTY keyboard or an AZER keyboard. When you click start, the game asks if you are a peaceful mind or a tortured mind. Giving your client this option can give insight into their mood.

In the first level, creatures tell you, "Don't let the mind's many horrors... extinguish your fire." Small, black creatures will try to hurt you, so you need to kill them with your fire before they can touch you. Each level prompts you to search, and you and your client have to work together to find clues. The aspects of teamwork and protecting each other make this a great game for building rapport.

Gun Mayhem Co-Op

Suggested Age Group: 10 and up

Therapeutic Benefits: Teamwork, aggression work, emotion regulation, planning and strategy

Telehealth Benefits: Many kids enjoy games involving guns and shooting, making this an ideal activity for clients who would benefit from aggression work. This game has minimal graphics, so it does not show gore like other shooting games might. Children can work through their aggression without directing it at the therapist, and you and your client can fight a common enemy together.

Setup: Go to https://www.twoplayergames.org/game/gun-mayhem, share your screen, and grant your client remote control. Gun Mayhem Co-Op has two options for cooperative play:

1. **Campaign:** When you start the game, choose *campaign* rather than *custom game* in the opening menu. You and your client will fight AIs together on various levels with increasing difficulty. If you play through on your own first, your client can choose which level they want to play.

2. **Last Man Standing (Team Mode):** Choose *custom game* in the opening menu, click on *last man standing (team mode)*, and then select *continue*. You can then choose from a variety of maps on which to play the game. Once you select a map, make one team consisting of you and your client (Team A), with the other team consisting of AI bots (Team B). You can choose from a variety of settings, and the object of the game is to take down every member of the AI team while surviving. You can decide how many AIs you want to play against and either give yourself an advantage (the two of you versus one AI) or fight two AIs at once.

Character customization options are the same as the competitive version of this activity (Gun Mayhem) in that you can change your character's look by choosing a hat, shirt, gun, and player color. Each player can also choose a specific perk or to not have a perk. Perks include: faster speed, no gun recoil, extra ammunition, or extra grenades.

Player 1 uses arrow keys to move, [to shoot, and] to use bombs. Player 2 uses the W, A, S, and D keys to move, T to shoot, and Y to use bombs. However, there is an option to change the control keys, so you can customize this if your client has a specific preference. The last team standing wins the game.

Interplanetary

Suggested Age Group: 8 and up

Therapeutic Benefits: Teamwork, communication skills, strengths work, problem-solving

Telehealth Benefits: This cooperative game has many components, making it a great way to work through frustration in a cooperative setting. It is a great activity for kids interested in space.

Setup: Three versions of this game are available, so you can keep presenting new levels:

1. **Interplanetary Original:** https://www.twoplayergames.org/game/interplanetary

2. **Interplanetary 2:** https://www.twoplayergames.org/game/interplanetary-2

3. **Interplanetary 3:** https://www.twoplayergames.org/game/interplanetary-3

Similar to many other online cooperative games, this one involves two astronauts, one large and one small, who must work together to collect gems and return to their ship. They need to help each other and rely on each other's strengths to get through the levels successfully. The smaller astronaut uses the arrow keys to move, and the larger one uses the W, A, S, and D keys.

One unique component to this game is that each astronaut has a limited oxygen supply, presenting a time limit. Air tanks appear on many levels, so you can replenish your supply if you need more time, but this provides an added exposure for clients with anxiety about time limits.

In early levels, various challenges are presented, and you need to figure out which astronaut's strengths are needed. It is very likely that you will need to try several times before figuring out the solution, providing opportunities for problem-solving. For example, the larger astronaut can put out fires by stepping on them, while the smaller one will burn. However, the smaller astronaut can walk through lava, but the larger one cannot survive touching lava. You and your client must work together and communicate to get through each level, all while making sure you do not run out of oxygen.

Ironic Zombie

Suggested Age Group: 8 and up

Therapeutic Benefits: Teamwork, communication skills, social skills, problem-solving

Telehealth Benefits: This cooperative game involves teamwork from two characters you would not typically imagine working together: a zombie and a human. Kids with an interest in zombies or those who feel like "outsiders" in their peer group take a particular interest in this game.

Setup: Go to https://www.twoplayergames.org/game/the-ironic-zombie, share your screen, and grant your client remote control. The zombie character moves with the arrow keys, and the human moves with the W, A, S, and D keys. Your goal is to navigate various levels and overcome challenges by working together. The zombie has limited time to finish each level but can pick up extra time along the way. This adds a component of coping with anxiety around time limits.

Unlike many other cooperative games, the zombie and the human are not trying to get to the same finish line. The zombie wants to return to its grave, and the human is trying to get to an exit door.

Therapy Tip: This activity can reinforce the idea that we can help someone accomplish a goal even if it does not immediately benefit us. Additionally, because humans and zombies are not traditionally portrayed as friends, this opens up conversation about how your client can navigate friendships and practice social skills, even with those who might not directly share their interests.

Last Survivors

Suggested Age Group: 8 and up

Therapeutic Benefits: Teamwork, communication skills, strengths identification, problem-solving

Telehealth Benefits: This is another great activity that encourages you and your client to practice working together to solve problems. Since the two characters have different skills, the game opens up an opportunity to talk about different strengths and how your client might use their unique strengths to overcome challenges or to help others.

Setup: Go to https://www.crazygames.com/game/the-last-survivors, share your screen, and grant your client remote access. The game includes two characters who are trying to escape from a city following a zombie apocalypse. The larger character moves using the arrow keys and can smash through certain things with the down arrow, while the smaller character moves with the W, A, and D keys, and throws rocks using the S key. The smaller character can fit through smaller cracks, but the taller character can walk through shallow water due to their height. Decide who will play which character before starting the game.

As with many of these games, you can choose to play through the game beforehand to unlock different levels or play with your client and unlock new levels together. Additionally, each level has the option to collect three gears if you want an added challenge on top of being able to successfully complete the level. If you want to add a challenge, try to get all the gears on every level.

Lost Pyramid

Suggested Age Group: 8 and up

Therapeutic Benefits: Teamwork, communication skills, planning and strategy, aggression work

Telehealth Benefits: Unlike many of the cooperative games presented here, Lost Pyramid presents a split screen, so you and your client do not have to stay close together to complete each level, giving you an added element of freedom. This can make this a good game for clients who are still learning teamwork and communication because it is not as essential to success in this game.

Setup: Go to https://www.crazygames.com/game/the-lost-pyramid, share your screen, grant your client remote control, and decide who will be which player. The man is controlled with arrow keys, and the woman with the W, A, S, and D keys. Your goal is to collect information, maps, and ammunition as you navigate the level. Some enemies can be destroyed by jumping on them, and others need to be shot. You have to use your ammunition carefully so you do not run out. Each character has different goals on each level, so you can help each other by talking through your specific challenges rather than directly working together. This can empower your client to keep trying different solutions instead of having you step in. There are multiple levels of the game, which you can decide to unlock beforehand or do so with your client.

Therapy Tip: This game includes enemies, some of whom you can fight but others whom you need to avoid. This allows for discussion of times when your client can overcome a challenge or "fight back" against an "enemy" in their life versus when they need to walk away.

Mike & Munk

Suggested Age Group: 8 and up

Therapeutic Benefits: Teamwork, communication skills, planning and strategy, taking turns, strengths work, frustration tolerance

Telehealth Benefits: Unlike many of the other cooperative games presented in this section, the two characters in this game do not move simultaneously. Therefore, in addition to working together to solve the various levels, you have to communicate and decide who will move and when. You must take turns rather than both moving about the level at the same time.

Setup: Go to https://www.crazygames.com/game/mike-&-munk, share your screen, and grant your client remote control. Both characters can be controlled either with the arrow keys or the W, A, S, and D keys. In addition, the X or J keys can be used to flip levers. The space bar toggles between the two characters. In this game, Mike (the human) and Munk (the squirrel) work together to escape a dungeon.

Each level presents unique challenges, including spikes, guns, and blocks. The squirrel can squeeze into smaller areas, but the human can jump higher. This opens up discussion about strengths and weaknesses. Additionally, neither character can finish the level until both make it to the door, again encouraging teamwork and cooperation.

Some levers and buttons that open up your path out of the level are time-limited (for example, a button will open a door for only a few seconds), so you and your client must also time your escape path carefully. If either character dies, the level restarts, giving you the opportunity to work through frustration in real time.

Miners' Adventure

Suggested Age Group: 7 and up

Therapeutic Benefits: Teamwork, communication skills, asking for help, planning and strategy, strengths work

Telehealth Benefits: This game has fun puzzles to solve in which players must gather specific resources rather than fight enemies. As with many cooperative games, the two players have different traits, which opens the door for talking about our unique strengths and how to best communicate to help each other solve problems.

Setup: Go to https://www.crazygames.com/game/miners-adventure, share your screen, and grant your client remote control. There are various levels you can choose from, though they need to be unlocked in order to access them. The man is controlled with the arrow keys, and the woman is controlled with the W, A, S, and D keys. You and your client need to move together, and if one character leaves the screen, they cannot move again until the other character joins them. Therefore, you have to communicate and work together rather than focusing exclusively on your own task.

The game provides instructions as you play, so the way to solve various puzzles is to find the appropriate directions. If you get stuck, it is easy to start the level over. Although both players have weapons and ways to break through barriers, they cannot accidentally hurt themselves or each other, which can make this game less frustration-inducing than some other options. Each player also gets three lives per level, so you can continue play after a mistake.

Money Movers

Suggested Age Group: 8 and up

Therapeutic Benefits: Teamwork, communication skills, problem-solving, exploration of emotions, strengths work

Telehealth Benefits: This game can be particularly engaging for kids who feel like they are "troublemakers" or who are frequently punished for their behaviors. They often relate to the role of a prisoner or someone who wants to escape from being in trouble. This game can open up the discussion of beliefs that they are a "bad" kid.

Setup: Go to https://www.crazygames.com/game/money-movers, share your screen, and grant your client remote control. This game involves two prisoners working together to escape prison. The taller prisoner moves with the arrow keys, and the shorter one moves with the W, A, S, and D keys. The taller prisoner can move heavier objects and lift the shorter prisoner, while the shorter prisoner can jump higher and squeeze into smaller areas. They must both use their unique strengths to complete the level. Some levels include security cameras or guards, so you need to hide to avoid detection to win each level. In addition to clearing each level, you steal money from the jail as you go for an added challenge.

For clients who have cleared all the levels but want to keep playing, you can also play the following versions:

1. **Money Movers 2:** https://www.crazygames.com/game/money-movers-2

2. **Money Movers 3:** https://www.crazygames.com/game/money-movers-3

3. **Money Movers Maker:** https://kizi.com/games/money-movers-maker

Space Prison Escape

Suggested Age Group: 8 and up

Therapeutic Benefits: Teamwork, communication skills, strengths work, exploration of emotions, problem-solving

Telehealth Benefits: As this is another prison escape game, clients with problem behaviors who identify with the role of a "prisoner" may find this game more engaging than some of the other cooperative games. It also has a science fiction angle that appeals to many kids' interests.

Setup: To play, go to https://www.crazygames.com/game/space-prison-escape (or https://www.crazygames.com/game/space-prison-escape-2 for Space Prison Escape 2), share your screen, and grant your client remote control. The girl moves with the W, A, S, and D keys, and the boy moves with the arrow keys.

This game is similar to Money Movers in that the players work together to escape from prison, but in this game, one of the prisoners is presented as female, making this game more appealing to clients who prefer to play a character of their own gender. In this game, the shorter character (the girl) can jump higher, double jump, and fit into smaller spaces, while the taller character (the boy) can move heavier objects. You and your client decide who will play which character and work together by playing on both sets of strengths to solve each level.

Zombie Mission X

Suggested Age Group: 10 and up

Therapeutic Benefits: Teamwork, communication skills, problem-solving, strengths work, frustration tolerance, planning and strategy

Telehealth Benefits: This is a fun cooperative game with cute animations that draw kids in. Although it involves fighting zombies, the graphics aren't scary or gory. Its aesthetics and controls are similar to other video games, so kids can figure out how to play pretty easily. Kids who are interested in fighting games can explore this interest while working cooperatively and practicing their communication skills.

Setup: Go to https://www.twoplayergames.org/game/zombie-mission-x, share your screen, and grant your client remote control. One player uses the W, A, S, and D keys to move, and the other uses the arrow keys. The game provides instructions as you go, so you can learn various skills while playing the game. The two players also share many skills, allowing you and your client to teach each other how to overcome challenges. At the same time, the two characters have some different abilities—for example, only one can crawl through small, low spaces—so you still have the component of strengths-based work.

In this game, you need to collect cookies, save people, and fight zombies. The cookies are not connected to the zombie theme, but since kids enjoy sweets, this can engage them and motivate them to work through the levels with you. Instead of lives, you each get a health bar, which you can replenish using potions that you can find around each level. The zombies also respond to your location rather than moving randomly, so you need to strategize to avoid them and ensure your safety.

Zoom-Be

Suggested Age Group: 8 and up

Therapeutic Benefits: Teamwork, communication skills, strengths work

Telehealth Benefits: Unlike the other zombie games presented in this section, this game involves trying to escape from scientists doing experiments on you. This game can be particularly engaging for kids who see themselves as outsiders, "weird," or different from their peers. It can also prompt conversation about feeling stuck or trapped.

Setup: Go to https://poki.com/en/g/zoom-be, share your screen, and grant your client remote control. Decide who will be the larger zombie and who will be the smaller zombie. The larger zombie can kick down walls, while the smaller zombie can jump higher and crawl into smaller spaces. The larger zombie moves with the arrow keys, and the smaller zombie moves with the W, A, S, and D keys. The goal of the game is to work together to overcome various challenges and capture all three stars in every level.

In addition, both players can boost each other to help overcome challenges. This creates a setting where your client can practice asking for, offering, and receiving help in real time. As with many cooperative games, the different skills of each player also allow you to work on identifying unique strengths.

Part **3**

Brain Games

Kids enjoy being challenged (sometimes), and brain games provide an opportunity to challenge them in a fun and safe environment. These games are not competitive and tap into skills around strategy, problem-solving, and overcoming challenges. Since these activities are more fluid, they provide a fun alternative to cooperative or competitive games if your client is not interested in following game rules or taking turns. Your client can work on the brain game on their own while you observe and narrate, or you can work together to solve it. Either way, these activities will help clients learn that they can do hard things.

This chapter explores 17 brain game activities that you can implement with telehealth clients. Some of these games include telehealth puzzle activities, which open up even more options and ensure that you never lose puzzle pieces ever again! In addition, online puzzle games have significantly more variety than the physical puzzles in your office. As with the other sections, the activities included here also suggest therapeutic topics you can incorporate into session as your client works to overcome the challenge presented.

Beautiful Mind Games

Suggested Age Group: 8 and up

Therapeutic Benefits: Problem-solving, frustration tolerance, executive functioning, focus, planning and strategy

Telehealth Benefits: This game offers several puzzle activities, some of which your client completes on their own with your support and help, and some of which you can play together. There are many options here that can be played in person, but as with all telehealth games, you will never misplace your pieces.

Setup: Go to https://www.crazygames.com/game/beautiful-mind-games and select a puzzle activity. The available activities are:

1. **Turbo Tiles:** In this game, you are trying to match either the corners or the sides of tiles to make a pattern. You can choose how complex you want the puzzle to be, from x-small, small, medium, and large. Click on the tiles to rotate them until you have matched all of the tiles.

2. **Numerica:** This game is like *Sudoku* in that it is a number-placement puzzle, and you must calculate and fill in the numbers that make the equations add up. This puzzle has timed and untimed modes, depending on your preference.

3. **Triomino:** For this puzzle, you are placing a series of three-square blocks on a grid (you can choose the size of the grid from 5×5, 6×6, or 7×7). When you place two squares of the same color next to each other, they will disappear. Your goal is to make the game last for as long as possible. You can see what block will appear next, which helps with strategy.

4. **Mind Shapes:** In this puzzle, you are presented with two 3D objects (cubes, cylinders, cones, etc.) in various colors (red, orange, yellow, blue, purple, etc.). There are five answers to choose from, and you must either select the object that exactly matches one of the choices, or the object that has neither color nor shape in common with either of the prompt objects. You can choose whether or not you want the task to be timed.

5. **Color Match:** You are playing on a grid with several colored blocks with stars on them. You have the power to change the background color, and any blocks that match the background color disappear. The goal is to make the whole grid one color. As with many of the puzzles in this section, the game can be timed or untimed.

6. **Roku-En:** You are presented with a series of cards with hollow or solid circles of various colors and in various positions. The objective is to match cards so that the hollow and solid circles match up. You can decide how many cards you want in each stack.

7. **Symbolica:** For this activity, you are trying to solve the puzzle in as few tries as possible. You can choose whether you want the puzzle to be x-small, small, medium, large, or x-large. Your goal is to match tiles that are horizontally or vertically adjacent to each other that have one thing in common, either the symbol or color (but that do not have both things in common). You can swap any two tiles on the board, meaning that tiles don't have to be adjacent to each other in order to move pieces around.

8. **Paranoia:** This game can be played in two-player mode with you and your client playing together. You are trying to form pairs by putting two pieces next to each other that share a shape or color (but not both). Pieces can be moved around, but with each move, you must create more pairs than you break. You can decide how large of a grid you want to play on.

9. **Memory Twist:** In this game, you are trying to find all of the stars on the grid. Any time you click a spot that does not contain a star, all the other stars disappear. You can try to memorize an x-small, small, medium, large, or x-large grid, and you can choose to play in twisted mode (where the grid rotates clockwise throughout the game) for an added challenge.

10. **Triangula:** This is similar to Making Squares from the competitive games section, but you are instead making triangles on a grid, and you choose how big the grid will be. You can play this in two-player mode and see who can make the most triangles. In one-player mode, you can decide how difficult you want the AI you are playing against to be.

Bomb Defuse

Suggested Age Group: 8 and up

Therapeutic Benefits: Focus, problem-solving, frustration tolerance

Telehealth Benefits: Puzzle challenges can be great in therapy, but physical puzzles typically have only one solution. This online bomb creator has dozens of puzzles that you can solve, with the difficulty increasing, so you can present it over and over. Plus, your client can create their own challenges, or you can create additional challenges for your client.

Setup: Go to https://www.crazygames.com/game/talking-and-nobody-explosion, share your screen, and grant your client remote control. There are seven levels available that vary in difficulty, and each difficulty level has multiple bombs. This means you can play the levels more than once, and it is not the same solution every time. You can also create custom bombs, so you and your client can create special challenges for each other. I suggest playing through a few times on your own because the instructions can be a little bit confusing. You want to ensure that you understand the task before presenting it to your client.

Bottle Flip

Suggested Age Group: 6 and up

Therapeutic Benefits: Focus, frustration tolerance, emotion regulation, teamwork, decision-making

Telehealth Benefits: Many kids enjoy playing bottle flip during in-person sessions, but some therapists are hesitant to do so due to the possibility of making a mess. The online version ensures that you'll be working in a mess-free environment, and the game has dozens of levels with various challenges to overcome.

Setup: Go to https://kizi.com/games/flip-bottle, share your screen, and grant your client remote control. You flip the bottle by clicking on it, and your goal is to flip it across a room by landing on various pieces of furniture and décor without letting it touch the floor. When I have used this game in sessions, I alternate levels, with the client completing one level and then me completing another level. I use my turns to model emotion regulation and frustration tolerance when I am having difficulty.

However, you can also allow your client to have greater control over how they approach the activity. For example, if your client is having a particularly difficult time completing a certain level, they can ask you to do part of a level but let them finish it. Others want to do all the levels and just ask me for help when it is needed. Allowing your client to make these small choices in a fun setting helps them practice making micro-decisions (small choices that do not have a set "right" answer), which can help them make decisions in other settings (What do you want to wear? Which snack do you want to eat?).

Dadish

Suggested Age Group: 8 and up

Therapeutic Benefits: Attachment work, frustration tolerance, communication skills, exploration of relationships

Telehealth Benefits: Dadish is a one-player game, so it is not one that you and your client play together. However, clients who are hesitant about doing therapy but enjoy video games can really engage in this activity, making them more likely to feel comfortable opening up.

Setup: Go to https://poki.com/en/g/dadish, share your screen, and grant your client remote control. Dadish centers around a father radish whose children have gotten lost and are in unsafe situations. He has to face enemies and overcome obstacles in each level to bring his children home. The game starts with a short clip that presents this background story, which the client can skip by pressing the enter key. The game then starts with a walkthrough, which shows how you can release Dadish from the dirt with the space bar and move him with either the A and D keys, or the left and right arrows. Pressing the space bar makes him jump, and he can double jump by double pressing the space bar. You can alternate playing levels, let your client play while you talk with them, or have your client take control but ask for help as needed if parts of the game get too challenging.

Therapy Tip: This activity has brought up great attachment-related discussion, especially with kids who have been separated from their parents for various reasons, including foster care or deployment. They can talk through missing their parent, the feelings they have about being apart, or the difficulties they've experienced adjusting to the parent's return (if this has occurred). If they are uncomfortable talking directly about their own situation, the story within the game gives them a safe space to explore these themes without having to acknowledge how the situation applies to their own life.

Find in Mind

Suggested Age Group: 4 and up

Therapeutic Benefits: Focus, executive functioning, impulse control, frustration tolerance, working memory

Telehealth Benefits: This activity presents various mini games to choose from, so your client can try many different tasks within this one activity. The tasks are all timed, which can allow you to work through any anxiety that your client has surrounding timed tasks. These brain games strengthen various executive functioning skills, including focus and working memory, and unlike in-person memory games, the prompts are different every time you play. The game uses simple colors and prompts, and each activity presents instructions when you start, so it is easy to learn how to do each one.

Setup: Go to https://www.coolstreaming.us/arcade/566/find-in-mind/ and click on the icon for the U.S./U.K. version of the game. Then share your screen and grant your client remote control. There are more than a dozen brain games to choose from, all of which have the common goal of finding a particular object. You might have to choose an object that does not belong, find an object that has the most matches, identify matching pairs of objects, or remember what you have seen before.

Your goal is to complete as many prompts as possible in the time provided, with a minimum set by the game. Each activity has many levels, with the prompts getting more difficult after you have cleared previous levels. If you make a mistake, a new prompt generates, and mistakes do not count against your total score. At the end, though, only your successful attempts are counted and not your mistakes. This can help kids keep trying tasks that are initially difficult for them. You can choose to do some of the activities with your client and model regulation when you make a mistake as well.

Find It/Hidden Objects

Suggested Age Group: 4 and up

Therapeutic Benefits: Executive function, focus, frustration tolerance, impulse control

Telehealth Benefits: I used to keep *Where's Waldo* books at my office for kids to look at while waiting for their appointment, but long-term clients would complain that they had already solved all of the books we had available. The online version of this activity provides a steady stream of new content, keeping it fresh and exciting for clients. Plus, the online version has a timed feature that allows clients to work through anxiety about timed tasks.

Setup: Go to https://www.hiddenobjectgames.com/, share your screen, and grant your client remote control. There are a variety of games to choose from that involve searching for hidden clues, objects, numbers, or letters, depending on your client's interest. Each game plays soothing music while you try to find all the targets within a certain time limit. If you guess incorrectly, you lose time, so your client must stop, think, and make sure they are choosing a target item rather than simply clicking impulsively.

If your client enjoys emojis, you can also do this activity at https://www.crazygames .com/game/emoji-hunt using the same setup. The client is tasked with finding one specific emoji in a crowd, with levels increasing in difficulty every time they find a target item.

Hexa Parking

Suggested Age Group: 6 and up

Therapeutic Benefits: Planning and strategy, problem-solving, focus, frustration tolerance

Telehealth Benefits: This activity reminds me of a puzzle ball I have in my office. The ball has several holes, each with a different color ring around it. It is filled with smaller colorful balls, and the object of the activity is to get each smaller ball in a hole that matches its color. This activity follows a similar concept but involves trying to move cars into the parking space that matches their color. My physical puzzle ball gets a lot of wear and tear and needs to be replaced often, which is not a problem with this virtual game. Plus, kids who like cars enjoy games that incorporate that interest.

Setup: Go to https://www.crazygames.com/game/hexa-parking, share your screen, and grant your client remote control. The game presents six parking spaces in different colors: red, yellow, green, blue, purple, and black. Your goal is to get each car in its corresponding space, leaving the black space open. Each space can contain only one car at a time, so the challenge is figuring out how to navigate each car to the correct space, with levels increasing in difficulty the more you play. The activity is simple to learn but difficult to master and can challenge clients to regulate their frustration while solving a difficult problem.

Hole

Suggested Age Group: 7 and up

Therapeutic Benefits: Problem-solving, frustration tolerance, focus, planning and strategy

Telehealth Benefits: This activity can help engage clients who like video games. Because the server may have other players who impede the client's progress, this can create opportunities for managing frustration in real time. Additionally, the platform is different every time you play, keeping it interesting and engaging for the client.

Setup: Go to https://hole-io.com/, share your screen, and grant your client remote control. In this game, your client assumes the role of a sentient hole in the ground that travels around the city and tries to get bigger by consuming more objects in its path. If there are other players on the server, your client can grow by consuming holes that are smaller than theirs. (But this also means your client can get swallowed by other players' holes!)

Your hole moves wherever you point the mouse. When your hole goes underneath a smaller object, that object falls into your hole and is consumed. As the hole consumes objects, it gets bigger and can consume larger objects. Some objects fall over before going into the hole, so you have to be big enough that they do not get stuck sideways. If this happens, you have to consume smaller items that fit around the blockage until you are big enough to consume whatever is blocking the hole. Each round is about two minutes long, and you can try again as many times as you want. More instructions appear when you load the website.

Therapy Tip: This game lends itself to many moments that you can make therapeutic. For example:

1. As your client progresses, they are able to consume things that they were too small to take on before (e.g., at first you can only consume things like manhole covers or people who are walking, but later you can consume trees and cars, and then buildings). You can use this aspect of the game to talk to your client about things they were previously unable to do and have since overcome, and discuss what supports helped them get there.

2. If your client gets swallowed up by another player, sit with that frustration and process the emotions associated with losing the game in real time.

3. As the hole consumes things on the screen, ask your client about things they "consume" or take in (e.g., music, television shows, social media) and how these things become part of them.

Mastermind

Suggested Age Group: 8 and up

Therapeutic Benefits: Focus, problem-solving, executive functioning, taking turns

Telehealth Benefits: As with many telehealth activities, there is an in-person version of *Mastermind*, but the online version has no cleanup, and you do not have to worry about losing game pieces in your office. The telehealth version also has more color options than traditional *Mastermind*, so it can be a greater challenge. If your client struggles to make choices, though, you can agree to use only the top six colors to simplify things.

Setup: Go to https://p8fwe.sse.codesandbox.io/ to play this game. The website is simple but can glitch if you do not use it correctly, so here are detailed instructions for making it work:

1. You and your client should each pull up the home page in your own web browser. The top of the page will state "instructions for Mastermind online." Click the red button that says *play now*, and have your client click that as well.

2. Choose your room name. You and your client must enter identical room names (case sensitive), and you can each choose your own nickname. When you have chosen a room name and nicknames, click *enter room*.

3. Whoever clicks *enter room* first gets to decide if they are the Code Maker or the Code Guesser. The other person is prompted to wait until the other player has made their choice. Then both click *master the mind!*

4. The Code Maker is then prompted to "set code now!" Using the four-peg board in the upper left-hand corner of the screen, the Code Maker makes a code using any of the eight colors on the right-hand side of the screen. They can repeat colors if desired.

5. Once the code maker has finished making their code, they click the green arrow.

6. The site will then prompt the Code Guesser to guess the code. They can choose from the eight colors to create a code as their guess. When they have input their guess, they click the green arrow to submit the guess.

7. The Code Maker looks at the Code Guesser's guess and puts red and white pegs next to each guess to indicate the accuracy of the guesses. A red peg

means the guesser got a color correct and put it in the correct spot, while a white peg means they got a color correct but put it in the wrong spot. When the Code Maker has finished inputting the red and white pegs, they click the green button.

8. The Code Guesser makes a new guess based on the red and white pegs, and this continues until they crack the code.

9. If the Code Guesser gets all four colors in the correct spot, the Code Maker clicks the red Thumbs Up button on the screen. This means that the Code Guesser has cracked the code!

10. If the Code Guesser does not have the correct code after 10 guesses, this typically means they have lost the game. However, you can allow them to continue to guess if you would like to let them keep trying.

Therapy Tip: Assign an emotion to the red and white pegs. Ask your client to give an example of a time they felt that emotion for each red or white peg on the screen. For a more complicated emotions game, you can do the same with the eight colored pegs.

Pick Up Sticks

Suggested Age Group: 6 and up

Therapeutic Benefits: Focus, executive functioning, emotion regulation

Telehealth Benefits: The physical version of this game requires finger dexterity, which can be tricky for clients who struggle with fine motor skills. This makes the online version a great alternative, as it simply requires pointing and clicking the mouse or touch pad. It is quick and fun, and clients can practice self-regulation skills in real time if they struggle with the game, or they can problem solve and practice focusing on a task for a sustained amount of time.

Setup: Go to https://www.coolstreaming.us/forum/arcade/game/19855.html, share your screen, and grant your client remote control. You can choose from five difficulty levels: loser, rookie, average, expert, and master. The goal is to match pairs of identical sticks as quickly as possible, similar to a matching game. However, you are able to see all of the sticks as you play, so you can click on any two pairs as long as they match. You and your client can either take turns finding pairs or you can have your client complete the task as quickly as possible. The game times each round so you can see whether or not you're making progress.

Therapy Tip: Between rounds, check in with your client and have them name any emotions they are feeling, as well as how intense these emotions feel on a feelings thermometer (where 1 = not intense at all, and 10 = super intense). See how more challenging levels impact how they feel, and practice using de-escalation and self-regulation techniques when they cross a certain threshold on their thermometer. If your client has anxiety about timed tasks, you can treat this game as a type of in-vivo exposure by having them see if they can beat their best time.

Riddles

Suggested Age Group: 6 and up

Therapeutic Benefits: Problem-solving, logic, frustration tolerance, communication skills

Telehealth Benefits: While it is easy enough to incorporate riddles into your in-person sessions, one benefit of telehealth is that you have the option to look up YouTube videos of riddles and try to solve them together. Some videos rely on your ability to solve the riddle based on the words used, while others use visual clues, so you can decide which type of riddle you want to incorporate.

Setup: There many different online options for riddles, though I have found that Bright Side (https://www.youtube.com/c/BRIGHTSIDEOFFICIAL/videos) and 7-Second Riddles (https://www.youtube.com/c/7SecondRiddles/videos) have many great videos to choose from. They upload new content frequently, so there is always something new to try.

Regardless of the site you are using, you will need to share your screen and audio so you and your client can view the video together. Many of these videos present several riddles in a row, with time to consider the question before revealing the answer. You can use the time limits to emphasize quick thinking or pause the video and talk through possible solutions together. Either option can be beneficial, as some of your clients might benefit from adhering to time limits, while others might engage better knowing they can take their time coming up with an answer.

Roblox Potion Experiments
(Wacky Wizards)

Suggested Age Group: 10 and up

Therapeutic Benefits: Problem-solving, imaginative play, strengths work

Telehealth Benefits: Lots of kids really enjoy Roblox and are excited at the opportunity to share this interest with you. If you are not familiar or comfortable with the platform, this gives your client the opportunity to teach you how to use it, which can be great for building rapport. The potion experiments activity in Roblox lets you and your client play around with different ingredients and see what the various potions do.

Setup: Go to https://www.roblox.com. You have two options for using Roblox in your telehealth sessions: You can either (1) have your client bring up their account and share their screen so you can see what they are doing or (2) make your own account and join your client in the platform. It is up to you if you want to be more actively involved with your own avatar or focus exclusively on what your client is doing instead of figuring out how to control your own character at the same time. Whichever method you choose, you need to ensure that you and your client only communicate through your HIPAA-compliant telehealth platform and not through the Roblox chat, as that is not encrypted or confidential.

When your client (or you and your client) enters the game, you will find a table, cauldron, and various ingredients. You combine the ingredients into potions and consume them to see what they do. Some transform you, like turning you into a zombie or making you larger or smaller, and some just make a part of you larger or cause your character to glitch. Through trial and error, you can figure out which potions give you strengths and which you want to avoid. The game is a lot of fun and creates an opportunity for logical reasoning and imaginative play.

Therapy Tip: Ask your client to pretend that these potion effects happened to them in real life. How would they feel? What would they do? Discuss what "powers" they would want to get from these potions and why.

Simon

Suggested Age Group: 4 and up

Therapeutic Benefits: Focus, working memory, frustration tolerance, communication skills

Telehealth Benefits: The original *Simon* is an electronic game that challenges players to remember and repeat back different sequences of lights and sounds. Although you can use the original game during in-person sessions, with the telehealth version, you'll never run out of batteries again! This version of Simon will also keep going until players cannot remember the pattern.

Setup: Go to https://www.memozor.com/simon-games/simon-game, share your screen and audio, grant your client remote control, and click *play*. If you cannot grant remote control because your client's device is not compatible with this feature, you can also have your client instruct you on which colors to press and still use this activity without remote control.

Simon can be a one-player or two-player game. For one player, you can take turns repeating the pattern to see who can remember the longest pattern. However, you can also work together and make a strategy to help each other remember an even longer pattern. Communicate what parts each person will recall and how you will work together to approach this game.

You can choose if you want the game to play at an automatic speed, slow, normal, or fast, so you can tailor the difficulty to your client's ability and developmental level. Additionally, you can mute the site if you want to play just following the colors. It does not have a time limit like the physical version of the game, so you can take as long as you need to try to remember the pattern.

Snowman

Suggested Age Group: 7 and up

Therapeutic Benefits: Problem-solving, exploration of emotions, communication skills

Telehealth Benefits: This game is a variation on Hangman, which is a pretty morbid game to play with children when you think about it. Therefore, instead of slowly drawing a person being executed in this activity, you will be drawing a snowman. If you're able to use a whiteboard for this activity, the biggest advantage of telehealth is that you can easily clear the board and start over.

Setup: I use the whiteboard feature on my telehealth platform for this activity, but you can use any whiteboard platform. In a pinch, you can also use pieces of physical paper and hold them up to the camera. To begin, decide who will be in charge of coming up with the secret word and who will be in charge of guessing. Draw lines for each letter of the word you chose, or have your client do this if they chose the word. You can then take turns choosing and guessing the word. When it is your turn, choose words that fit in with the child's treatment plan or history, such as feelings words or coping skills you have practiced.

The first three incorrect answers represent the circles making up the snowman's body, followed by the two arms and the hat. You can always expand to include different parts of the face, buttons, and more clothing if your client is struggling to get the correct answer and you do not want them to lose. On the other hand, you can grant fewer wrong answers if one of your goals is to practice regulating emotions when they lose a game.

Tunnel

Suggested Age Group: 6 and up

Therapeutic Benefits: Mindfulness, motor skills, emotion regulation, frustration tolerance, patience, focus

Telehealth Benefits: Tunnel is similar to those old games where you try to guide a marble through the maze without it falling in the incorrect hole. It can be incredibly frustrating, but with practice, it gets easier. The visuals and music are very relaxing in this online activity, so it draws kids in and helps them self-regulate when they are having trouble.

Setup: Go to https://blackthornprod-games.itch.io/tunnel and share your screen, or have your client pull it up on their web browser and share their screen. (If you experience lag when your client has remote control of your screen, the game works better if they share their screen.) The game has two modes: basic and ultra. The difference is that ultra mode moves much faster and is more challenging. Since this is a one-player game, you can narrate your client's emotional responses, process their experience, and cue de-escalation skills as needed while your client plays.

In the game, you are guiding a small oval through a tunnel to a key on the other side. You must help it get there without touching the sides of the tunnel. If it touches a side, it explodes, and the level starts over. Once you click the mouse, the level starts, and the oval moves toward wherever you put the mouse. You have to focus and steer carefully to get through each level! The levels get harder as you go, so the game continues to challenge you and create opportunities for self-regulation and mindfulness work in real time.

Unfair Mario

Suggested Age Group: 8 and up

Therapeutic Benefits: Frustration tolerance, emotion regulation, working memory, communication skills

Telehealth Benefits: Incorporating video games into in-person sessions can be difficult, but they fit right in with telehealth sessions. Kids who are interested in Mario can get really engaged in this extra-challenging version.

Setup: There are two versions of Unfair Mario. Both involve sneaky, hidden challenges that make this game more difficult than regular Mario platforms:

1. https://www.unfair-mario.com/

2. https://iogames.onl/unfair-mario-run

Pull up the website you want to use, share your screen, and grant your client remote control. Although the game tracks how many tries it takes you to get through a level, there is not a limit to how many lives you have. Your client will most likely "die" many times, creating real-time opportunities to de-escalate and practice frustration tolerance skills. They will also have to remember where the threats are and what sequence gets them through each part of the level, which means this game helps them practice their working memory muscles.

Therapy Tip: If you would like, you can take turns each time Mario dies. With this method, you can model frustration tolerance for your client when you die, and you can encourage them to practice asking for help when they are having a hard time. You can also let your client try the level repeatedly as you narrate their emotional experience via their facial expressions (for example, "I notice you are making an angry expression" or "You are clenching your jaw like I do when I feel frustrated") and prompt them to use their skills.

Wonderfully Juicy

Suggested Age Group: 8 and up

Therapeutic Benefits: Problem-solving, impulse control, focus, emotion regulation, patience, mindfulness

Telehealth Benefits: This game has cute animations and relaxing music, making it enjoyable and engaging for kids, and the setup opens the door for therapeutic conversations as you play.

Setup: Go to https://blackthornprod-games.itch.io/wonderfully-juicy, share your screen, and grant your client remote control. The object of the game is to get a certain number of gummies into the juicer, with each level presenting different challenges. You can alternate levels or work together to solve each one.

Each level has controls to let you generate the gummies and move them to the juicer. Gummies come out of the pipe at the top of the screen whenever you click on it, with one gummy generating with each click. Each level has different controls that you can manipulate, marked with white arrows and lines, which make it easy to figure out what is expected each time.

Some levels have obstacles you have to avoid that can destroy the gummies before they get to the juicer. There is a limit to how many gummies you can generate on each level, and you have a goal number of gummies to get into the juicer. This means that you can make a mistake and still complete the level, but you have to be careful because you can run out of gummies.

Therapy Tip: The following are some therapeutic themes that come up with this activity:

1. Each level gives you more gummies than you need to reach your goal, which allows for mistakes and learning opportunities. If you mess up, you can still reach the goal for that level. Ask your client about a time in their life when they made a mistake but were able to fix it.

2. Every level presents a different obstacle between the gummies and the juicer. Have your client talk about a goal they have and what obstacles have gotten in the way.

3. On some levels, you must time your movements in order to successfully clear an obstacle. Have your client sit with any feelings of impatience or frustration that come up from having to wait or having to start over due to incorrect timing.

4. Have your client attempt a particularly difficult level on their own. See how they manage feelings when they struggle to do something. Explore how it feels to need to ask for help or to be unable to complete the level on their own.

5. Have your client imagine that the gummies are a big feeling they had recently. Have them share what the feeling was and how they "juiced" the feeling (coped and brought the feeling down). They can also share a time when they did not successfully bring the feeling back down and what happened then.

Part 4

Creative Activities

Children are incredibly creative, and tapping into this creativity with expressive activities can lead to amazing things in a therapy session. It can allow clients to express a part of themselves they were not comfortable sharing through traditional talk therapy, or they might tap into something they did not even realize was there. As long as clients have art supplies available, they can engage in almost any artistic or creative writing activity over telehealth. They can simply hold up their creation to the camera for you to see or read it to you when it is done.

However, clients from low-income families might not have access to some supplies, and you and your client cannot do a joint drawing task together using physical art supplies. Additionally, if an art project is deeply personal or private to the client, they cannot leave it at your office where you can guarantee that no one else in the family will see it. For these reasons, most of the creative activities in this chapter are device-based. Use your clinical judgment to determine when it's appropriate for a client to use their own supplies.

Other creative, hands-on play activities can be done over telehealth if the client has that specific toy in their home, but again, this is not always an option, and you and the client cannot do the task together. Most of the activities described here do not require that the client have any specific toys on hand, but you have the option to use their toys in a session if you deem it clinically appropriate. In this section, you will find 18 telehealth activities that involve creating and building.

Buddha Board

Suggested Age Group: 6 and up

Therapeutic Benefits: Mindfulness, relaxation, creativity

Telehealth Benefits: A Buddha Board is a canvas that can be drawn or painted on with water, and as the water dries, whatever you created fades away. While it is a great therapeutic tool, the material is delicate and can scratch easily if you are not gentle enough with the paintbrush. Also, if you touch it with your fingers, the oil on your hands can ruin it. With a virtual Buddha Board, these concerns are not relevant. The virtual Buddha Board also fades at the same rate every time, so you do not have to wait as long. You can also change the color of the pen.

Setup: This activity works using the Zoom whiteboard feature. Your client has to be the one to share the whiteboard on their screen. When they bring up the annotate options, they need to select *spotlight* and *vanishing pen*. With this virtual Buddha Board, there is no final product because their creation disappears as they make it. This allows your client to focus on their emotional experience of creating rather than on trying to make the product look a certain way. It also helps them to relax and let go of their inhibitions because whatever they make will disappear, no matter how they feel about it.

While the activity itself creates a relaxing environment to practice mindful awareness and relaxation skills, you can also use it to foster discussion about self-forgiveness, as the disappearing drawing can be seen as a metaphor for "letting go" of something they have done in the past. You can also prompt your client to draw something that scares them or makes them angry to show that difficult things can pass.

Character Creator

Suggested Age Group: 8 and up

Therapeutic Benefits: Identity development, insight building, strengths work, goal setting

Telehealth Benefits: Drawing a self-portrait is a common projective art therapy tool that therapists use in session, but some clients struggle because they do not think their artistic skills are "good enough" for the task, and they get caught up in their picture not turning out exactly how they want it to. Some also struggle with not knowing where to begin. This task provides a template with choices, which makes it accessible for those who prefer not to draw or who need options as a starting point.

Setup: The site I use for this activity is https://charactercreator.org/, although many options come up when you search for "character creators" or "character generators." I like the options presented by Character Creator, though I wish they had more options for gender and body type. To begin the activity, share your screen and grant your client remote control. A good standard prompt for this activity is "I want you to make a character of yourself." However, the options are limitless, including:

1. "I want you to make a character of who you want to be when you grow up."

2. "I want you to make a character of the best version of you."

3. "I want you to make a character of yourself on a very bad day."

4. "I want you to make a character of your best friend."

5. "I want you to make a person who is _____." (insert whatever adjective relates to the client's needs: strong, smart, happy, angry, sad, etc.)

6. "I want you to make each person in your family."

You can also simply prompt them to "create a person" and let them take that in whatever direction they want. Sometimes depersonalizing a task like this allows the client to dig deeper into their own thoughts and values since they have the protective layer of "but this is not really about me" to distance themselves from any uncomfortable feelings that might arise.

Regardless of the prompt you use, have your client personalize their character or characters to their exact specifications, including clothing and accessories. You can narrate throughout the task to notice any themes in your client's creations. If you want to explore deeper, you can ask the following questions when they are finished:

1. Who is this person?

2. What is this person good at?

3. What does this person need help with?

4. Who takes care of this person?

5. What does this person like to do?

6. What does this person hate to do?

7. Where does this person live?

The options are endless! Through these questions, your client can further explore their identity, build insight, notice their strengths and areas for improvement, and set goals for their future.

Choose Your Own Adventure

Suggested Age Group: 8 and up

Therapeutic Benefits: Narrative work, creative expression, exploration of emotions, identity development, communication skills, trauma processing, decision-making

Telehealth Benefits: Narrative work has an important place in therapy, particularly for clients who are struggling with trauma, navigating identity issues, or working to understand their emotions. In telehealth sessions, it is easy to use computer programs to organize these stories and put them together in a way that is comprehensive and easy to review. For this activity in particular, being able to rearrange and reorganize images and aspects of the story makes telehealth a particularly helpful method of service delivery.

Setup: Creating a choose-your-own-adventure story over telehealth can be done a number of ways. Google Slides and Canva make it easy to put together slide shows of story options, though saving things to these platforms is not HIPAA-compliant. If the story might contain identifying information about your client, you will need to use PowerPoint, Publisher, or Word on your hard drive to do this work.

I recommend using programs on your device, screen sharing, and letting the client put things together using screen control rather than having them save their stories on their own device. This is because children and teens often use shared family devices, and parents, siblings, or even friends might see what they saved. Use your clinical judgment to determine whether it is appropriate to let them save it on their end or if the risk of someone seeing it could be harmful to them.

Choose-your-own-adventure stories tend to be extensive and in-depth, so this activity could take several sessions. You can save your progress and pick up where you left off at the next session. If your client's attention span is limited, you can also work on it in chunks for part of a session. The following section provides you with some guidelines on creating and sharing these stories, including considerations for more client-directed or therapist-directed stories.

Creating Stories: All stories start with an introduction that gives the reader background on the characters and events. For this activity, a good story structure includes points at which your client needs to decide between two actions for their character, as this keeps the story from getting too complicated and presents them with two clear options.

A simple story (good for younger clients) can have three points at which your client makes a choice. As demonstrated on the figure below, this would lead to eight possible endings:

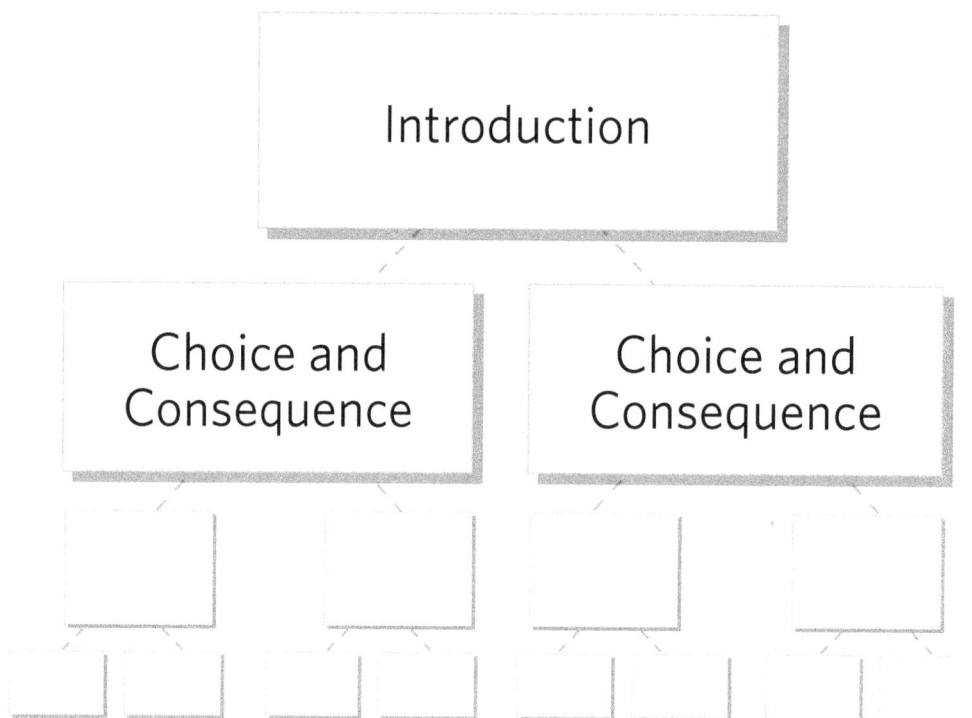

```
                    ┌─────────────────────┐
                    │    Introduction     │
                    └─────────────────────┘
              ┌───────────────┐   ┌───────────────┐
              │   Choice and  │   │   Choice and  │
              │  Consequence  │   │  Consequence  │
              └───────────────┘   └───────────────┘
          ┌────┐      ┌────┐   ┌────┐      ┌────┐
          └────┘      └────┘   └────┘      └────┘
        ┌──┐  ┌──┐  ┌──┐  ┌──┐  ┌──┐  ┌──┐  ┌──┐  ┌──┐
        └──┘  └──┘  └──┘  └──┘  └──┘  └──┘  └──┘  └──┘
```

Older clients (or those who really enjoy writing and narrative-based activities) might create more complex and longer stories with several possible endings. You can also create choice "loops" where one set of choices brings the reader back to an earlier choice. This can be helpful if your client has behavioral goals in their treatment, as it gives them the opportunity to go back and make a different choice the next time.

Client-Directed Stories: You may want to take an open-ended approach to this activity, giving your client complete control over how the story unfolds. In this case, ask them what they want their story to be about. They might choose to base the story on something that has happened to them, or they might create a fictional story. Either option is fine, as you can pull themes from the story and apply them to your client's treatment goals where appropriate.

Therapist-Directed Stories: Alternatively, you might choose to present your client with a story structure that is already laid out if there is a specific topic that you want to cover or if your client struggles with making choices. In this case, you will want to have an introduction prepared before the session begins. I find it works best to create an introduction that is unique to the client so you can address that client's specific needs. Topics for a therapist-directed story might include:

- A fantasy story about an anthropomorphized animal who goes on an adventure

- A story about a character who deals with a social conflict

- A story about a family who experiences something difficult or stressful together

- A character who has a positive experience with their family

- A story that pulls an experience from the child's life

Sharing the Narrative: Once your client completes the activity, you can go through the story together, seeing how different choices affected the ending and making parallels to your client's own life. You can also see what components of the story were not within the main character's control and use this as a starting point to discuss how we sometimes have to accept things that are out of our control. If appropriate, your client might want to share their story with a parent or guardian as well. You can let the parent or guardian make decisions as your client shares their story with them to demonstrate how adults make choices as well.

Color by Numbers

Suggested Age Group: 6 and up

Therapeutic Benefits: Creative expression, release the need for control, following directions, exploration of emotions, perfectionism, patience

Telehealth Benefits: Color-by-number worksheets can be a great therapy tool for clients who experience a strong need for control. When you're using physical worksheets, though, the client can still deviate from the instructions and color in the picture using whatever colors they want. With this telehealth version, they have to follow instructions in order to complete the picture. This creates a unique opportunity to work through perfectionistic tendencies and the need for control while engaging in a creative task.

Setup: Bring up https://iogames.onl/color-by-numbers, share your screen, and grant your client remote control. They are presented with dozens of pictures to choose from. When the image loads, they can zoom in on the image to see where each color is supposed to go. As mentioned, they can only place colors with the assigned number, so they have to follow instructions in order to complete the image.

The images are broken down into pixels, and your client must fill each pixel with the appropriate color to complete the image. This can bring up feelings of frustration or impatience, which you and your client can work through together in real time.

As your client works on their drawing, you can talk through just about anything, but you can also ask them about the emotional experience of doing a task that requires them to do something in a predetermined way. When they finish the drawing, you can save the image and send it to them to remind them that they got through it!

Coloring Book

Suggested Age Group: 4 and up

Therapeutic Benefits: Creative expression, relaxation, perfectionism, exploration of emotions

Telehealth Benefits: Clients who struggle with perfectionism often respond well to computerized drawing tasks that prevent them from going outside the lines and allow them to undo anything they perceive as a mistake. While it is important to work through the client's self-critical tendencies, the following virtual coloring activities can help build rapport and increase your client's comfort with therapy before you transition to other interventions that specifically address perfectionism. These sites make it easy to engage in drawing tasks with your client, regardless of their age, developmental level, and interests.

Setup: For the coloring page websites below, pull up your chosen website, share your screen, and grant your client remote control. Your client can choose what image they want to work on in the session and engage in the drawing task.

1. **Google Art Coloring Book:** Go to https://artsandculture.google.com/experiment/art-coloring-book/1QGsh6vSfAQBgQ. Described as an experiment, this website offers iconic images from art and culture. You can match colors to the original or make your picture with any colors that you choose. Sections include texture and shading, making the resulting image look incredibly realistic.

2. **Online Coloring:** Go to https://www.online-coloring.com/. Great for young kids, this website has simple coloring pages and many color options to choose from. The website offers a simple process to save, print, or share the final product if your client wants to keep a copy.

3. **The Color:** Go to https://www.thecolor.com/. This is another site that has a lot of options young kids might enjoy. Coloring pages are sorted by category, so clients can look for options based on their interests and preferences. There are a wide variety of pictures that vary in intricacy, so clients can also decide how challenging they want the activity to be or how detailed they want their coloring pages to be.

4. **Coloring Online:** Go to https://www.coloringonline.com/. This website is great for middle or high school-aged clients (or even adults!), as it offers complex mandalas and other complicated coloring sheets. In addition to

several coloring options, this website lets you create custom colors that clients can tweak to their exact preferences and needs.

5. **Coloring Book:** Go to https://coloringbook.pics/. This site has a wide variety of options available, from simple, child-like pages to more detailed "anti-stress" coloring pages. Like Coloring Online, this site also lets you mix custom colors.

Once your client is more comfortable talking with you in sessions, and you feel it is appropriate to start working on perfectionistic tendencies around coloring inside the lines or making mistakes, you can transition to using freeform coloring pages. You can search for any images that appeal to your client by using a search engine. Share your screen, and let your client pick out what coloring page they want to do. They can then work on their coloring page in one of two ways:

1. **Paint:** If your device has a Paint program, you can copy and paste the image onto a blank document. Share your screen and grant your client remote control. They can use the preloaded colors or create their own custom colors to fill in the picture.

2. **Whiteboard Fox:** Go to https://r2.whiteboardfox.com, click *start drawing*, select *draw and erase anything* and *expires in 14 days*, and then click *create whiteboard*. The website will generate a unique link you can share with your client, and they can join you in the private room. Click *options* and then *add pic*, and you can upload an image file of the client's preferred coloring page. The Whiteboard Fox platform allows you and your client to work on the drawing simultaneously, so you can work together on the picture. You can also upload two images and engage in parallel drawing where you and your client each work on your own coloring page simultaneously. However, limited color options are available on Whiteboard Fox, so the client might prefer the wider range of options that Paint offers.

Comic Strips

Suggested Age Group: 8 and up

Therapeutic Benefits: Identity development, exploration of emotions, communication skills, creative expression, narrative work

Telehealth Benefits: Many kids and teens find therapeutic benefit in creating stories or short comics about their feelings or the issues going on in their lives, but some who feel that their artistic skills are not good enough might hesitate or feel uncomfortable drawing the images themselves. One great thing about computers is that clients can use clip art or pre-loaded images instead of having to create their own. Pre-existing templates also simplify the creative process.

Setup: Canva (www.canva.com) has countless templates available for comic strips. One that I really like to use is "Colorful Blob Love 6 Panel Comic Strip," which you can find by using the search bar at the top of the website. (You can prompt your client to only use the top three panels if they prefer or if the activity calls for it.) The template includes shape characters, facial expressions, and accessories, which allow your client to create unique characters to express different emotions or experiences.

For younger clients, you can prompt them to create a three-panel comic detailing something that happened to them in Panel One, how they responded in Panel Two, and how everything turned out in Panel Three. You can explore the interaction between their feelings and their behaviors, as well as the connection between their actions and consequences.

A more non-directive approach to this task is to let your client create any story that occurs to them. They can use all six panels if they need to (or even add more!), and when they finish, they can share their story with you. You can explore themes and emotions that arise and discuss how these might fit with your client's treatment goals. You can also connect the story to any issues your client is experiencing outside of the session. If appropriate, they can then share their story with a parent or guardian.

Creating a Sensory Space

Suggested Age Group: 6 and up

Therapeutic Benefits: Sensory soothing, relaxation, mindfulness

Telehealth Benefits: When I see in-person clients, I sometimes recommend creating a sensory space in the home, especially for kids who need help self-regulating. I will tell the family what a sensory space looks like and make suggestions for how to put it together. With telehealth, the client can make the sensory space during their session, and I can see what they have created and actively be a part of this creative process.

Setup: Depending on the client's age, it might be appropriate to have the parent or guardian join you for the session. If the sensory space will be a permanent fixture in the home, make sure that the location, size, and objects used for the sensory space are appropriate and approved by the guardian. Have the client bring their device to the location in their home where they plan to create their sensory space and encourage them to explore what comfort items they want to include in this space. Common items they might want to consider include:

1. Soft blankets or pillows

2. Weighted blanket

3. Stim or fidget toys

4. Soft lighting (or maybe "galaxy lights")

5. Stuffed animals or other comfort items

6. Sounds that they find relaxing

The items available might vary depending on the client's socioeconomic status, so I encourage clients to create their own list of comfort items that they already have. If they want to purchase items for their sensory space, I encourage the parent or guardian to sit with the child and put together a wish list based on what is accessible and affordable for the family. You can devote one session to creating this list (and then put the space together the following week) or do both tasks in one session if all needed items are in the home.

When all of the items are present, talk the client through the process of setting up the space in a way that is comfortable for them. A good sensory space has privacy, so if possible, it should be in a private room or even a closet. They can also use blankets or furniture to make a fort to use as a sensory space.

Once the sensory space is created, ask the client how they feel when they are in the space. Have them process what emotions they feel in their body, and do a guided relaxation exercise to help them feel safe and comfortable in the space. Then educate the parent or guardian on the purpose of the sensory space, explaining how this space is meant to help the client de-escalate and get their sensory needs met. You want to prevent any misunderstandings and ensure that the space is used appropriately. Access to the sensory space should not be time-limited, nor should it be taken away if the client gets into trouble for misbehavior.

Diamond Art

Suggested Age Group: 6 and up

Therapeutic Benefits: Creative expression, mindfulness, relaxation, patience

Telehealth Benefits: Diamond art and diamond painting have recently increased in popularity, especially among kids. However, it is not always feasible to do this in your office. Physical diamond painting requires you to have a lot of supplies on hand and can make a big mess. Plus, it can be frustrating for your client if they make a mistake and the art does not turn out the way they were hoping. Telehealth diamond art has no clean up, no potential to run out of diamonds or have pieces go missing, and the paint-by-number setting prevents mistakes.

Setup: Go to https://www.bestgames.com/Diamond-Painting-Asmr-Coloring or https://www.yiv.com/Diamond-Painting-Asmr-Coloring (both websites are the same game with the same levels and images). The game will only load if your ad blocker is disabled, so make sure that it is paused or turned off before bringing up the website. Share your screen and grant your client remote control. All your client needs to do is match the diamonds to the corresponding numbers in the image.

Each level of the game involves a different picture, and levels are unlocked when you complete the previous level. If you want your client to be able to choose what picture they want to make, I suggest playing through before using this game in a session. It is quick and simple to make each of the pictures, so you can do this quickly.

Therapy Tip: As your client does the activity, you can process how they are feeling and turn this into a mindfulness exercise. You can also present this as something for your client to focus on as they sit with you, keeping them engaged in the session but still leaving enough brain power to have a conversation about their treatment goals, behaviors they have had this week, or conflicts they have experienced.

Dream Home Design

Suggested Age Group: 8 and up

Therapeutic Benefits: Goal setting, identity development, creative expression, guided visualization, exploration of emotions

Telehealth Benefits: This is an excellent activity to help clients think about their future and picture what they want to see for themselves as they grow up. The software used for this activity allows the client to create their space in a visual way, allowing them to physically see how they want to manifest for their future.

Setup: Many options are available for creating home designs online, with different benefits to each. The following are two different options I have found useful.

Planner 5D: Go to https://planner5d.com/editor, share your screen, and grant your client remote control. Your client can choose if they want to design a home from scratch or use a pre-made template. Template options for rooms are: bathroom, bedroom, empty room, or kitchen and living room. Templates for living spaces are: studio, two-story house, apartment, and office.

When you start the project, it takes you through the basic controls, so your client can quickly learn how to navigate the program. They can choose to view each room in 2D or 3D, and they can customize every aspect to their exact preferences, including how many rooms they want in their house and what they want to have in each room. Various furniture, furnishings, and landscaping items are available.

Although many options are only available if you purchase the premium version of the software, there are also choices that you can access for free. You can save projects so your client can work on their dream home across multiple sessions. (Just make sure you save the project with a code rather than your client's real name for privacy purposes!)

Home By Me: The setup is the same for this platform—simply go to https://home .by.me/en/, share your screen, and grant your client remote control. Although this site has similar controls and tutorials as Planner 5D, it does not have any pre-made templates your client can use as a starting point. However, one positive of this platform is that there are many more furnishing options that you can access for free. Again, you can save your progress and let your client return to their project at a later date if they run out of time in their session.

Therapy Tip: As your client creates their dream home, talk with them about their choices. How many bedrooms are they including? What does this mean about who they want to have live in their dream house with them? What kinds of furniture are they choosing? Soft? Industrial? Are they choosing bright colors or more muted tones? What are your client's priorities for their home? What makes them feel safe, comfortable, or "at home"? Process these things as they create their space.

Lite Brite

Suggested Age Group: 4 and up

Therapeutic Benefits: Mindfulness, relaxation, creative expression

Telehealth Benefits: Never worry about a light bulb burning out again with the telehealth version of Lite Brite! Even very young kids can engage with this activity because there is no choking risk from small parts, and they will never run out of the color they want to use or have pieces go missing.

Setup: Go to http://www.happydaric.com/lite-brite/, share your screen, and grant your client remote control. They can create whatever freeform light image they would like by choosing from the colors provided. The one drawback of virtual Lite Brite is that your client cannot use a light-by-numbers sheet to help them with a specific design, but this gives them the opportunity to be creative by making an image from their own mind or developing an abstract image. You can save the final product by taking a screen shot.

Therapy Tip: Prompt your client to make an image based on an emotion and have them create the image using colors they associate with that emotion.

Magnet Poetry

Suggested Age Group: 8 and up

Therapeutic Benefits: Creative expression, narrative work, exploration of emotions, communication skills

Telehealth Benefits: Unlike a physical magnetic poetry set, the benefit of telehealth is that there are unlimited words! The online version allows you to load more options if you feel stuck or want a word that is not on the page. When you reload the word list, it leaves the words you already selected but drops more options to choose from.

Setup: Go to http://magneticpoetryplayonline.com/original/, share your screen, and grant your client remote control. They can then create magnet poetry from any of the words presented. In my sessions, I prefer to take a non-directive approach to this task and let the client create whatever type of poem reflects what they feel, want, and need in that moment.

Check in and process the emotions your client is experiencing while doing this task. See how different words resonate with them and what kinds of words they are choosing. Is their poem very visual? Are they choosing emotion words? The creation itself speaks volumes and is incredibly therapeutic, and it also opens doors to further therapeutic conversation. When they are finished, you can save the poem as a PNG file and keep it for reference, send it to your client, or both.

Joint Poetry Writing: Create a poem with your client, having them alternate with you in choosing words, or alternate writing lines. This can be a great activity for groups as well, with everyone in the group working together to write the poem.

Marble Run

Suggested Age Group: 8 and up

Therapeutic Benefits: Planning and strategy, executive functioning, focus, problem-solving

Telehealth Benefits: I have a physical marble run set in my in-person office, but I constantly lose marbles under couches or behind desks. My clients will also occasionally step on a piece and break it, resulting in missing parts of the set. These are all things that do not happen online! In the telehealth version, the laws of physics are also very precise, so the marble follows a specific route, making problem-solving and troubleshooting much easier. Not only that, but the telehealth version can shoot the ball upward or teleport it to another part of the track, giving you significantly more construction options than you have with the physical version.

Setup: Go to https://www.marblerun.at/, share your screen, and grant your client remote control. It can be a bit of a learning curve to discover how each part moves and interacts with other components, but this is all part of the fun. This activity works well in one-on-one sessions, but you can use it in a group format by having each member take turns adding to the run to create something together. The website also has a gallery feature where you can play with tracks made by other users or share your track when it is finished. Since the site does not require identifying information to submit your track, sharing your client's track will not violate their confidentiality.

Therapy Tip: If you want to use this activity to get your client talking more in-depth about their treatment goals or symptoms, you can establish prompts or questions for when they use a certain block or for each time they run the ball through the track.

Plot Generator

Suggested Age Group: 8 and up

Therapeutic Benefits: Narrative work, creative expression, exploration of emotions

Telehealth Benefits: Narrative work can be very powerful, but some clients become overwhelmed and do not know where to start. This plot generator activity gives them a jumping-off point. They can, of course, update and change the resulting plot to meet their needs.

Setup: Go to https://www.plot-generator.org.uk/story/, share your screen, and grant your client remote control. Go through the options together, and have your client fill in the type of story they want, including the characters, the emotions they want portrayed in the story, and their preferred ending. The site will generate a story based on their preferences. If a basic story does not capture your client's interest, the website has options for other genres of stories, including crime, fairytale, science fiction, dystopian, and many others.

Unfortunately, this website only offers male/female options for character gender, and it defaults to he/him pronouns if you do not choose a gender. This means if your client's pronouns are something other than he/him or she/her (or if a character in their story has other pronouns), you will have to go through the story and manually change it.

Because parts of the story are written in Mad Lib style, you might end up with a pretty hilarious story, which serves to build rapport with your client as you read through it. Plus, if they are having trouble deciding what word to use, there is the option to have the generator suggest a random word that fits into that category. This keeps the activity low-pressure, which I find particularly helpful for anxious clients who worry about choosing the "wrong" word or sounding "stupid."

Therapy Tip: When the generator asks your client to name a place where the story happens, ask them where they wish they could visit. When it prompts them for various adjectives to use in the story, ask them to choose adjectives that describe someone they care about. When it asks them for emotion words, ask them how they were feeling when a specific event occurred. For example, "How did you feel on your vacation?" or "How did you feel when you got grounded?" There are endless ways to personalize this activity! Once the story is done, process it with your client and have them articulate how it is similar to and different from their own experiences.

Timeline

Suggested Age Group: 10 and up

Therapeutic Benefits: Narrative work, goal setting, exploration of emotions, trauma processing, strengths work

Telehealth Benefits: This is a variation of an activity I learned as a practicum student, in which clients either write or draw out a timeline of what their life was like in the past, what it is like today, and where they hope it will be in the future. When using this activity in telehealth sessions, clients can still draw or write their timeline on a physical piece of paper if they choose, but they can also use the whiteboard feature, PowerPoint, Canva, or another virtual template. This allows for more creative expression and can help clients who feel shy about their drawing skills better engage with the activity.

Setup: Present your client with the following three prompts, or with any variation that feels appropriate. You can either present all three at once or one at a time:

1. "I want you to imagine your life five years ago [or a different length of time if appropriate]. Think about where you lived, who took care of you, and who the important people in your life were. Think about what things you were good at and what things you needed help with. Think about what you wanted to see change as you got older and what you wished were different. Write or create that."

2. "Now, think about how your life is today. Where do you live and who takes care of you? Who are the important people in your life? What are you good at and what do you need help with? What are you happy with and what do you wish were different?"

3. For the third prompt, you can use either of the following scripts. Remember to change the time range as appropriate. I typically use the same time range for the first and third prompt, as this is easier for the client to remember.

   a. "Next, I want you to picture what you think your life will be like in five years. Try to guess what will happen based on what is going on for you now. Who will the important people in your life be? What things do you think you will be better at? What things do you think might still be hard for you? What will be different from now, and what will be the same?"

   b. "Next, I want you to imagine what you want your life to be like in five years. If you could decide what happens next, what would change?

What things would you get better at? Who would still be important in your life? Is there anyone you might prefer not to have around? What is different from your life now? What is the same?"

Use your client's responses and the timeline they create as a starting point to work on their goals for the future, build insight into how their past experiences have affected them, and identify their strengths. Where appropriate, this activity can be used in discussions of trauma history.

Vision Boards: Challenges

Suggested Age Group: 8 and up

Therapeutic Benefits: Creative expression, problem-solving, exploration of emotions, communication skills, goal setting, behavioral activation, strengths work

Telehealth Benefits: Vision boards can be a great resource for goal setting and behavioral activation, and the telehealth setting makes for smoother organization and layout. Clients can change the board easily and without "messing up" anything else on the board. They also have access to a wider range of images and fonts because they are creating the board on a computer and can search for images that meet their exact specifications and needs. (For the purposes of creating a vision board in therapy that will not be displayed anywhere or sold, you can use copyrighted images.) Furthermore, because this task involves identifying challenges, the client can easily destroy or delete challenges they have overcome to represent their progress.

Setup: I like to use Canva (www.canva.com) for vision board activities because templates are readily available, and many images are pre-loaded onto the platform. However, if your client wants to use images or words that might be identifying, you may want to use PowerPoint and only save their work to your encrypted hard drive. You can use an image search to pull whatever pictures your client wants to use. Depending on your client's device, you can screen share and grant them remote control, or you can have them screen share so you can view what they are putting together.

For this activity, you can choose to have your client create a vision board that represents past or current challenges. If you choose a past orientation, have your client list three things (or more, if appropriate and time allows) that were very difficult for them to overcome, but that they have successfully gotten through. Have them find images, affirmations, art, or anything else that represents what happened *and* what got them through it (including skills that they have or people who supported them). This will help them identify their strengths and support system.

If you choose a future orientation, have your client name one specific challenge they are currently facing. (It is easiest with this activity to focus on one challenge at a time—if your client is dealing with multiple challenges, you can always do this activity more than once.) Have them create a board of what they are going through and what resources they will use to overcome this challenge, including affirmations, coping skills, personal attributes, their support system, or any other positive asset.

Once your client is done with their vision board, you can save it for use in future sessions. However, remember to determine whether it is appropriate, confidential, and safe for your client to save the final product on their own device—this will be a case-by-case decision.

Vision Boards: Life Goals

Suggested Age Group: 8 and up

Therapeutic Benefits: Goal setting, behavioral activation, strengths work, creative expression

Telehealth Benefits: As noted previously, online vision boards make for smoother creation, easier editing of existing boards, and faster access to endless photographs, drawings, artwork, and any other images your client wants to include on their board.

Setup: Use your preferred platform for making vision boards (Canva, PowerPoint, etc.) and either share your screen or have your client share theirs. Prompt your client to create a vision board that represents three goals they want to accomplish. (You can use a lower number if your client struggles to come up with three, or set a higher number if appropriate.) Set a time frame for achieving these goals that is developmentally appropriate for your client, such as six months, one year, five years, and so on.

As your client works to create their vision board, make sure their goals are clear and actionable by discussing what specifically it is that they want to do, what it will look like when they are successful, and what steps they need to take to get there. Talk with them about additional supports they might need or changes they might have to implement in order to make these goals a reality. You can also address barriers that are not within your client's control. Sit with these frustrations and identify how your client can know when a barrier can be overcome and when they might need to make adjustments to their strategy.

Vision Boards:
What Makes Me Happy?

Suggested Age Group: 6 and up

Therapeutic Benefits: Emotion processing, creative expression, coping skills, guided imagery

Telehealth Benefits: As with the other vision board activities listed in this chapter, the telehealth setting is ideal for creating and modifying vision boards and allows access to infinite images that your client can use for the activity.

Setup: Set up your chosen vision board platform (Canva, PowerPoint, etc.), and either share your screen or prompt your client to share theirs, depending on what you decide is most appropriate. Ask your client to explore how happiness, joy, or excitement feels in their body, and then ask what images, thoughts, or ideas come to mind when they imagine feeling that way. Have them create a vision board based on these ideas.

Once your client creates their board, they can print a copy of their vision board (if it is safe and appropriate to do so) and hang it in a place where they can look at it whenever they want to have a happy thought. Your client can also practice visualizing the images from their vision board and go to this space in their mind whenever they need to de-escalate.

Vision Boards: Who Loves Me?

Suggested Age Group: 5 and up

Therapeutic Benefits: Attachment work, exploration of emotions, self-esteem

Telehealth Benefits: Unlike a physical vision board, clients can revisit and modify their virtual boards without having to start over. You also don't have to print images or have any additional supplies on hand, as clients can simply pull images from the internet or social media to incorporate into their project.

Setup: Bring up your preferred vision board platform (Canva, PowerPoint, etc.) and either share your screen or have your client share theirs. Tell your client that they will be creating a vision board to represent the people in their life who love and care for them, including family members, friends, caregivers, teachers, and other trusted grown-ups. They can also include representations of things that make them feel loved, like images from a trip they took or a special gift they received.

This activity can be especially impactful for kids with behavior issues. Often, kids who act out don't realize that people still love them even when they are having a hard day. This activity can open the door to talking about unconditional love and help them see that they are still loved and lovable even in those hard moments.

Part **5**

Just For Fun

Sometimes, kids don't want to play games that have a predetermined end goal, nor do they want to do a task that requires them to create something specific. In these moments, it can be helpful to engage them in a non-directive activity that they simply enjoy, such as pretend play, dress-up, creative exploration, or virtual reality. These activities do not require clients to have a specific outcome in mind, but they allow you to build trust by making the session a space where they have control. Additionally, non-directive work can allow children to process emotions in a nonverbal manner.

In this section, you will find 12 non-directive therapeutic activities that help clients relax and develop self-regulation skills in a fun, laid-back way. These activities can help them identify coping skills they can use when their feelings get too big and allow them to regulate within the session itself. As they explore each activity, they can notice how they are feeling and identify which activities bring different emotions up or down in their bodies. Some activities simply present an opportunity to build rapport, as they give your client something enjoyable to focus on while they engage in a conversation with you about a deeper issue.

Bop It

Suggested Age Group: 5 and up

Therapeutic Benefits: Focus, executive functioning, following directions, frustration tolerance

Telehealth Benefits: Bop It is a great game for helping kids learn how to follow directions as they follow a series of voice commands. The biggest benefit of playing the virtual version of Bop It is that it has subtitles. Clients who are hard of hearing, have auditory processing issues, or struggle with focus seem to benefit from being able to read the prompts in addition to hearing them.

Setup: Go to https://arcade.gamesalad.com/games/151323, share your screen, and grant your client remote control. Decide whether you want the subtitles on or off and whether you want the standard "bop it, twist it, pull it" options or whether you want to add a "shake it" option for an extra challenge. The game speeds up, so it gets more challenging the longer you play. You can play cooperatively with your client, with them being in charge of some prompts and you being in charge of others, or you can take turns and see who can last the longest without missing a prompt.

Dress-Up

Suggested Age Group: 5 and up

Therapeutic Benefits: Identity development, decision-making, creative expression, non-directive play

Telehealth Benefits: So many dress-up games are available online, with endless possibilities, including Disney princesses, anime characters, historical figures, cartoons, pets, angels, demons, and just about anything else you can imagine. My in-person dollhouse has limited options for dressing up the characters the way that my client wants, so these telehealth versions allow for deeper identity exploration than in-person sessions. Additionally, the various accessory options are laid out in each game, so the client does not have to dig around and search for the piece they want.

Setup: As mentioned, there are hundreds of dress-up games available for free online. Some that I have used in the past include (but are not limited to):

1. **Doll Divine:** https://www.dolldivine.com/ (This site also has a "random" button that will choose an activity for you if your client is struggling to make a decision.)

2. **Dress Up Games:** https://www.dressupgames.com/

3. **Dress Up Who:** https://www.dressupwho.com/

4. **Girl G:** https://www.girlg.com/dress-up-games.html

Pull up the website you want to use, share your screen, and grant your client remote control. As your client dresses up their character, you can talk with them about their choices and see how they identify with the character or what they prioritize when dressing up their character. Unlike in-person versions of playing dollhouse, the emphasis in these telehealth games is on dressing the character rather than setting up a dollhouse or engaging in imaginary play in the house. This allows you to use the activity to help your client practice making small decisions about what they will choose for each aspect of the game. These micro-decisions can be challenging for both adults and kids, so this activity allows your client to practice this skill in real time.

Ducklings

Suggested Age Group: 6 and up

Therapeutic Benefits: Attachment work, focus, exploration of relationships

Telehealth Benefits: This activity does not have an exact parallel for in-person sessions, making it a great telehealth offering. In the activity, you pretend to be a duck that is swimming around in a lake, and you collect babies to take back to your nest as you go. Plus, as clients play, they unlock new hats, including a lily pad hat and an eggshell hat, that their duck can wear!

Setup: Go to https://iogames.onl/ducklings-io, share your screen, and grant your client remote control. The object of the game is to swim around a pond, collect baby ducks, and bring them safely home. The duck moves wherever you point the mouse, and ducklings follow you in a line when you swim near them. The ducklings can be anywhere, so clients might have to search the same area multiple times to find more. As they bring the ducklings home, they unlock more features in their nest—for example, the nest gets bigger and more colorful—and collect new hats. When all the ducklings arrive home, the duck co-parent expresses love and happiness that the babies are back!

Therapy Tip: Since this game requires clients to assume a loving parental role that can parallel or contradict their own life experience, it can get clients talking about their own attachments, especially to parents or guardians. If your client has ever been separated from their caregivers, ask them what it was like and how it felt when the caregiver returned (or explore how they feel now if they are not currently in their caregiver's care). Talk about what their caregiver does to keep them safe or times when they did not feel safe. You can also discuss what their caregiver could do to help them feel safer.

Extreme Speedboat Driving

Suggested Age Group: 6 and up

Therapeutic Benefits: Frustration tolerance, emotion regulation, relaxation, non-directive play

Telehealth Benefits: Much like playing with matchbox cars in your office, this activity is a fun, non-directive way to engage with your client. Kids who enjoy video games can build rapport with activities like this because it taps into an existing interest and falls outside of what they might expect that therapy "should" look like. Learning to manage the game controls also helps them practice frustration tolerance and work on getting better at a skill.

Setup: Go to https://www.crazygames.com/game/speed-boat-extreme-racing, share your screen, and grant your client remote control. Select *free drive* and *2P mode* (you can choose the *1P mode* option if your client will be engaging in the activity independently while you narrate). Select your boat and your client's boat. Player 1 is controlled with the W, A, S, and D keys, and Player 2 is controlled with the arrow keys.

The platform has obstacles you can try to navigate, or you can simply drive around the lake enjoying yourself. I find that activities like this one can be a way to decompress in the final minutes of a session where you have processed something intense and heavy, allowing your client to regulate, orient back to the present moment, and be ready to leave the session.

Filters

Suggested Age Group: 4 and up

Therapeutic Benefits: Imaginative play, non-directive play, creative expression

Telehealth Benefits: Similar to playing dress-up in your office, using virtual filters allows you and your client to take on a disguise or wear a mask in your session. They are great for pretend play, which allows young children to process their emotions in a developmentally appropriate way. You can also use filters to approach difficult topics in a depersonalized and non-threatening way.

Setup: If you use Zoom for your telehealth sessions, filters are available under *Video Settings* and then *Backgrounds & Filters*. There are a few basic lighting filters available, but for the purposes of imaginative play, there are several to choose from. You can wear sunglasses, various hats, or a mask; make yourself into a bunny, unicorn, shark, bear, or other animals; or put yourself on a television screen or on stage at a theater. Under *Studio Effects*, you can also change your eyebrows, add facial hair, or wear lipstick. I have used the lipstick function to turn my lips blue when a client wanted to pretend we were at the North Pole to simulate looking cold.

Therapy Tip: As a non-directive intervention, the specifics are up to you and your client. I follow their lead and narrate play as I would if we were in person, reflecting any emotions and themes as I notice them.

Get Over It

Suggested Age Group: 6 and up

Therapeutic Benefits: Frustration tolerance, emotion regulation, letting go

Telehealth Benefits: This game has cute animation and simple controls that pull the child in. Its design is such that the controls are difficult to master, and the game remains challenging even if you have played for a while. It creates real-time opportunities to regulate and bring down frustration and other strong emotions.

Setup: Go to https://www.crazygames.com/game/getting-over-it, share your screen, and grant your client remote control. Click on *New Game* to begin playing. The client will use their mouse (or finger if using a device with a touch screen) to help the cat move across the screen. To move, the cat must overcome various obstacles by pulling itself up with a hammer. This activity can be incredibly therapeutic because it draws out big emotions, including frustration. You can use a feelings thermometer to track your client's emotions as they play, and encourage them to practice using coping skills once their emotions start to cross a certain threshold on the thermometer.

Therapy Tip: The title of the game lends itself to therapeutic processing of emotions. Ask your client what things they are holding onto that they want to "get over." For example, was someone unkind to them and they are carrying a grudge? Are they holding onto an unfairness or injustice that occurred? Explain to the client that although anger can sometimes be a motivating force, if they are dwelling on an issue without making wanted changes, it can keep them stuck. You can also normalize not having to "get over" everything by helping the client sit with their feelings and then identify how they can channel those feelings into positive action.

Good Vibes

Suggested Age Group: 6 and up

Therapeutic Benefits: Mindfulness, relaxation, emotion regulation

Telehealth Benefits: This activity is simple, relaxing, and aesthetically pleasing. It can be a great tool to help a child regulate themselves after processing something difficult, allowing them to be in a good place emotionally at the end of the session.

Setup: Go to https://blackthornprod-games.itch.io/good-vibes, share your screen, and grant your client remote control. In this activity, your client simply clicks through a series of planets with flowers, smiling faces, and friendly creatures, some of whom give positive affirmations as they play. To move, your client simply clicks on the translucent circles that surround each planet. If you follow the line of planets, you reach a *Next* button. This takes you to more planets with different colors and affirmations. If desired, you can take turns, but the object of this activity is to let your client relax and prompt them to share what feelings come up for them as they do the activity. It is simple and easy, and there is not a set end to the activity, so they can jump around for just a few minutes or for a longer period of time if they want to.

Nature Cams

Suggested Age Group: 5 and up

Therapeutic Benefits: Relaxation, attachment work, exploration of emotions, focus, communication skills

Telehealth Benefits: If you have ever wanted to take a therapy field trip to the zoo, now you can! With the internet, you and your client can live stream just about any animal, from dolphins to polar bears. You can tie in your client's favorite animal to their session and observe the animal's behavior as a way to work on identifying emotions and social skills. You can also simply observe the animals when the client needs to de-escalate and relax before transitioning back to the rest of their day.

Setup: You can search for various live streams online. The one I use most frequently is https://www.explore.org/livecams because there are so many animals and types of streams to choose from. Share your screen, and let your client choose what animals they want to observe. This site has streams of birds, aquariums, pet rescue centers, and various animal sanctuaries. Most display live streams, so you get to view their behavior in real time (meaning you might have to manage disappointment if an animal does not come out or is taking a nap during your session time). However, some have preset reels of highlights. For example, there is a puffin nest camera that loops footage of the mother caring for the babies. (This particular video is great for attachment work.)

Therapy Tip: Have your client tell you a story of the animals on the screen. Who are they and what do they want? What are they doing and how do they feel? Have them create a narrative about the animals and identify thematic elements that tie into the client's own experience.

You can also ask clients to guess what emotions an animal might be experiencing based on their behavior during the live stream. Have your client describe these emotions and specify how they came to that conclusion. Then, talk about a time that your client felt that way.

Paper Airplanes

Suggested Age Group: 6 and up

Therapeutic Benefits: Frustration tolerance, problem-solving, emotion regulation, autonomy, mindfulness, following directions

Telehealth Benefits: Kids love making paper airplanes, and I have used this activity both in my in-person office and in telehealth sessions. While it can be appropriate and therapeutic to encourage kids to ask for help when need it, the telehealth version of this activity forces the client to complete the task without your help. They will need to practice listening, following instructions, and focusing on the task in order to build their plane. This can build autonomy and is a perfect opportunity for real-time emotion regulation.

Setup: Most of the telehealth activities I use do not require the client to have any supplies on hand other than their smartphone, tablet, or laptop. This makes the activities accessible regardless of the resources the client has on hand or the family's socioeconomic status. However, for this activity, they will need plain printer paper. I have found that most clients are able to supply this, but if this is not the case, I simply choose a different activity for that client.

Share your screen, and search YouTube for video tutorials of paper airplanes. If you are using a tutorial with verbal instructions, make sure you have also shared your audio with the client. Usually, I let my client decide which airplane they want to create, but you can assess the difficulty level and redirect your client to something simpler if they are drawn to something particularly complicated.

You and your client will each make paper airplanes by following the tutorial. Check in with your client about their progress, particularly any feelings of frustration or irritation that arise when they encounter a difficulty with the task. Since you are meeting via telehealth, you cannot step in and make the airplane for them, so you will have to help them work through these feelings and problem solve any parts they find challenging. However, if they are able to follow the directions successfully and overcome these difficulties, they will have an awesome paper airplane at the end of the session!

Role-Plays

Suggested Age Group: 10 and up

Therapeutic Benefits: Decision-making, identity development, exploration of emotions, narrative work, understanding consequences

Telehealth Benefits: Role-plays are a great therapeutic tool to help clients practice various life skills. In this virtual role-play activity, clients will create their own choose-your-own-adventure story but with thousands of total choices and potential outcomes. The game follows a timeline based on the choices a client makes, and their character's personality is impacted by these decisions. This makes for great learning opportunities and opens the door to discuss any parallels with the client's own life.

Setup: The platforms I have used for this activity are Alter Ego (https://www.playalterego.com/) and Bitlife (https://fireboyand-watergirl.io/bitlife-life-simulator). Go to either site, share your screen, and grant your client remote control.

1. **Alter Ego:** Alter Ego is a life simulation game that starts in utero and goes throughout the lifespan. During each phase of development, the client can choose from a flowchart of events to have various experiences. The client can choose specific types of events if they want more of that kind of experience, but they will age out of a developmental period before they are able to go through every single option. As their character gets older, there are also side options that take up time. The client's relationships with other characters, their personality, and their financial status are all impacted by the choices they make. There is a set storyline for this game, so limited outcomes are available.

2. **Bitlife:** Bitlife starts at birth and randomly generates an identity for the client. As with Alter Ego, the choices they make in Bitlife impact their personality, relationships, and career options, but they also have to be mindful of their physical health in the game. It is more in-depth, and there is not a limit to how many experiences they can have or when they have to age into the next year. Some clients might find the options overwhelming, but others like having a higher level of control over the game. You can decide what is best for each client on a case-by-case basis. Additionally, if your client's character in Bitlife has a child, they can reincarnate as this child when they die.

Both Alter Ego and Bitlife include sexual themes at certain points in the story. They are text-based and not overly descriptive, but you want to make sure that this is appropriate for a given client before using this activity in a session. In addition, both of these games also only have the option for cisgender male and female characters, making the activity less than ideal for transgender or nonbinary clients. Alter Ego also only has the option for your character to be heterosexual, though you choose if you are a boy or a girl at the start. Bitlife randomly assigns gender but lets the client indicate their sexual orientation.

Roller Coaster VR

Suggested Age Group: 6 and up

Therapeutic Benefits: Body work, mindfulness, exploration of emotions

Telehealth Benefits: Many of us have used roller coasters as an analogy for how emotions can shift over time, but with this virtual reality version, the activity comes to life for the client. They can have a lot of fun pretending they are at an amusement park for their session while doing important emotion work.

Setup: A version of this activity is available for free on the Oculus store, but of course, this is only available if both you and your client own virtual reality (VR) headsets. However, you can still do VR roller coasters on any device that can play videos. Go to YouTube, share your screen (including audio), and search *VR Roller Coaster*. You can add words like *scary*, *underground*, or other adjectives to find a more specific experience. Make the video full screen, and pretend you are riding the roller coaster together. I also use a Zoom background that makes it look like I am riding in a roller coaster, which adds a nice touch but is not essential for the activity. As you ride the virtual roller coaster together, you can have your client identify what they are experiencing in their body, or you can just do this activity for fun and rapport building.

Therapy Tip: If you'd like to use this activity to help your client better explore their emotions, use the following emotional roller-coaster script:

"Sometimes our feelings are like a roller coaster. They can go up or down very quickly, and we do not always know what is coming or how we will feel as things happen around us. Imagine that this roller coaster represents your feelings, and your moods go up when the roller coaster goes up and down when the roller coaster goes down."

Then have your client provide examples of various times they have had roller-coaster emotions. You can use these prompts or come up with your own as appropriate:

1. When has your mood been really high?

2. When has your mood been really low?

3. When was a time your mood was up but went down very quickly? What happened?

4. When is a time your mood felt like it was going in loops, like you were going up and down very quickly?

5. What kinds of things "pull" you up out of a low mood?

Wish List

Suggested Age Group: 4 and up

Therapeutic Benefits: Communication skills, goal setting, identity development

Telehealth Benefits: I created wish lists with clients long before I started doing telehealth, usually around Christmas if this was a holiday that the child celebrated. This worked just fine, but the added benefit of telehealth is that you can pull up images of what the clients wants. You can also create a list on Canva using images of each item.

Setup: This activity can be done a number of ways. Platforms such as Amazon let anyone with an account create a wish list and set that list to private if they do not want anyone to be able to see it. If a specific retailer has many items that the client wants on their list, they can fill a cart through that website. You can also write a list in a Word document or on paper. Choose whatever option is most convenient and appropriate for your client.

There are several prompts you can use with this activity. You can simply let your client make a list of items they wish they owned, or you can specify that they are creating a list of items for their future home. (The latter can be a great supplement to the Dream Home Design activity and can help the client develop a future orientation.) Their wish list can include clothing and accessory items that match their personal identity or style. It can also include items that would help them with a hobby they want to pursue, help them achieve a future job they want to have, or help them reach a specific goal. Kids tend to have fun making the list, and the prompts you associate with it help them explore their identity and goals in a fun and non-threatening way.

Part **6**

Talk-Based Activities

Although many children process their thoughts and emotions through play-based activities, it can be helpful to use talk-based interventions if you are doing narrative work, providing psychoeducation, or practicing communication skills. While you might incorporate non-directive play or other child-centered activities in your session, talk-based activities are a great addition to work on specific skills. For instance, you can discuss coping skills that have worked for your client in the past or new skills they could use to handle similar situations in the future. Even the act of talking allows kids to work on their communication skills.

In addition, the activities in this chapter can help you teach kids how to express themselves in an appropriate way. Since young kids do not communicate or process in the same way as adults, they can struggle to share their feelings using words. They are also more likely to shut down if they are nervous or unsure, as opposed to verbally expressing what is happening for them. Therefore, this chapter includes 10 interventions to get clients talking, help them express and process emotions in session, and practice communication skills that they can use in other areas of their lives.

Chat: Secrets

Suggested Age Group: 8 and up

Therapeutic Benefits: Communication skills, trust building, exploration of emotions

Telehealth Benefits: Sometimes it is easier to share something by writing it down rather than having to say it. The benefit of using a typed chat feature is that you do not have to worry about deciphering your client's handwriting. Some clients with fine motor issues also find typing easier than writing, so this lowers inhibitions and makes the activity more accessible to them.

Setup: Show your client how to use your telehealth platform's chat feature. Explain that sometimes it can be easier to share things by writing them down rather than saying them out loud, and you want to see if they feel more comfortable sharing things this way. You also can give them the option to type something without sending it if they want to get a secret down but are unsure about sharing it with you. (This is another telehealth advantage: You cannot see what they are typing until they send it, so clients might feel freer knowing you are not reading as they write.)

Then take turns sharing secrets with your client. As the therapist, this entails a certain degree of self-disclosure on your part, so you should choose secrets that will help your client feel more comfortable in the session and normalize sharing. Be sure that you choose self-disclosures that do not involve any of your client's personal triggers, and focus on how these disclosures will help your client engage and share. As you explore what your client shares, ask them why this information is secret, why they don't want others to know about this information, and how they feel about the secrets.

Confidentiality Note: Before encouraging a client to share a secret, make sure that they understand any limits to confidentiality. For example, therapists have an ethical obligation to disclose if a minor client shares that they are being abused. If a client shares something that falls under mandated reporting—and they did not understand that you cannot keep that information confidential—this can harm the therapeutic relationship and also impact their ability to trust other adults in the future. Make sure that you explain the limits of what secrets you can keep before starting this activity, and answer any questions your client has about this before moving forward.

Emoji Reactions

Suggested Age Group: 4 and up

Therapeutic Benefits: Communication skills, exploration of emotions, mindfulness

Telehealth Benefits: Some kids really enjoy emojis, so much so that their text-based conversations will often involve emojis rather than the words. This activity incorporates that interest into your telehealth sessions while getting your client to explore their emotions with you.

Setup: If you use Zoom for your telehealth sessions, there is a "reactions" option next to the screen share button. You can search through hundreds of available emojis. If you use another platform, the chat feature might have emojis available, though you can also copy and paste in emojis from another website. (I have used https://getemoji.com/ for this.)

Present your client with different emotion words and have them assign an emoji to each word. The number and complexity of the words you use may vary depending on your client's age and developmental level. For very young children, I usually start with happy, sad, angry, and scared. You can also find feelings lists of varying lengths by searching online.

As the emotions get more complex, your client might pick two emojis to encompass one feeling. They also might represent a feeling with an emoji that does not involve a facial expression (like the fire emoji for anger). Have them explore their choices and how each emoji represents these feelings.

Mad Libs

Suggested Age Group: 6 and up

Therapeutic Benefits: Communication skills, exploration of emotions, creative expression

Telehealth Benefits: If you like to use Mad Libs games in your sessions, the biggest advantage of telehealth is that you will never run out of fresh worksheets. No matter how many times a client requests this activity, there is always a fresh version that they have not seen before. There are also word generators, so there is less pressure if they are struggling to think of an adjective, noun, or other word.

Setup: There are many free version of Mad Libs available online, and you can search for any that meet your specific needs. Websites I have used include:

1. https://www.madlibs.com/printables/ (includes PDF printables)

2. https://www.glowwordbooks.com/blog/category/kids-online-mad-libs/ (for elementary-age kids)

3. https://www.madtakes.com/ (with suggested words if you cannot think of one)

4. http://www.redkid.net/madlibs/ (includes traditional Mad Libs)

If you are using a website that has fillable boxes, you can screen share and have your client either tell you the words or have type them in themselves with screen control. If you are using the PDF printable site, you will want to write down your client's answers and wait to share your screen until the activity is complete.

Therapy Tip: Use a search engine to find worksheets that have emotion prompts, and ask your client to choose an emotion-based prompt that is related to something that happened to them recently. For example, "A noun that you are scared of" rather than simply "A noun." This activity lowers client inhibitions and opens the door to exploring their emotions in a non-threatening and fun way.

My Needs

Suggested Age Group: 8 and up

Therapeutic Benefits: Communication skills, exploration of emotions, mindfulness

Telehealth Benefits: When done in person, this kind of activity usually requires either you or your client to write notes. A major benefit to screen sharing is that you can both simultaneously look at the same worksheet, and the person who is not making notes can see what is written down in real time. Additionally, typed responses are easier to organize.

Setup: Before the session, create a fillable PDF using the sample worksheet on the next page. I have used https://www.sejda.com/pdf-forms and https://www.jotform.com/fillable-pdf-form-creator/ to create fillable PDFs for free. These platforms are not HIPAA-complaint, so you should not upload any document with protected health information. However, they can be helpful in creating a worksheet template you can use in therapy. You can save templates as a Word document or as a fillable PDF, depending on which works best for you.

When the session begins, share your screen and let your client know that you are going to do an activity that will help them understand their needs. I start by saying, "We all need help sometimes, but it can be hard to know what we need or to communicate those needs to the people around us. This activity will help you learn to express your needs in a way that adults understand." Then use the prompts on the worksheet to help your client articulate their needs in a healthy and appropriate way. I encourage you to develop client-specific prompts, but the sample worksheet provides examples that can be used as a starting point. I have found that many clients respond well to starting with a hypothetical scenario, as it is impersonal and does not apply directly to their lives.

My Needs Sample Worksheet

Jesse is out running errands with their mom. It has been a long day, and Jesse feels tired. Jesse's iPad is at home, and they want to play Minecraft with their friends. As they are walking in the grocery store, Jesse says, "Mom, can we go home now?" Jesse's mom says, "Not yet. We still have a few more things to get, and then we have to stop at the bank." Jesse's eyes fill with tears and they yell, "I want to leave *now!* You never *listen* to me!"

What do you think Jesse's needs are?

_____

_____

_____

_____

How could Jesse have let their mom know their needs more effectively?

_____

_____

_____

_____

How could Jesse's mom have addressed their needs differently?

_____

_____

_____

_____

Think of a time when you needed something but had a hard time expressing your need.

When was it?

_____

_____

_____

What was happening?

_____

_____

_____

How did you express the need?

_____

_____

_____

Did people understand what you were asking for?

_____

_____

_____

What could you have done differently?

_____

_____

_____

Pet Finder

Suggested Age Group: 4 and up

Therapeutic Benefits: Communication skills, social skills, exploration of emotions, self-esteem

Telehealth Benefits: I typically would not use a website like Pet Finder during an in-person session because I rarely use a computer when meeting with clients face to face. This intervention came to me by accident when I complied with a client request, thinking, *Let's see where this goes*. With the available pets changing every week, there are always new prompts for this activity.

Setup: This activity can be done with any website that posts information about available pets or animals, but I usually use https://www.petfinder.com/ because I am most familiar with it. Share your screen, and let your client choose the type of pet they would like to search for. There are usually more cats and dogs available than other animals, but you can search additional pet types if you would like. Scroll through the available pets, and have your client choose some from the photos. I often start with three, but you can do more if you would like.

Read through the biographies together, which typically include information about the animals' histories and personalities, and prompt your client to explore whether the animals they chose would get along well. Identify whether they have complementary qualities (for example, a very timid cat and a very protective cat could help each other) or whether their qualities might prevent them from being good friends. You can also have your client look at animals who are labeled as needing to be the only pet in their home. Discuss why the pet might do better by themselves and how they are still lovable and have good qualities even if they struggle to get along with others.

Photo Share

Suggested Age Group: 4 and up

Therapeutic Benefits: Communication skills, exploration of emotions, exploration of relationships

Telehealth Benefits: Depending on your therapy style and the boundaries you set in your sessions, your clients might not bring electronic devices such as phones or tablets to in-person sessions. Since most people do not carry physical photos with them anymore, this prevents you from doing photo share activities in sessions. With telehealth, your client can easily screen share and show you pictures. Plus, since you are both looking at the image simultaneously, you can view your client's facial expressions as they share the image with you.

Setup: Make sure that your telehealth platform settings allow for your client to share their screen. Younger kids might need a parent or guardian to help them with the screen share controls. Then prompt your client to show you a photo from the past week. This can be a photo of them or a photo that they took. This approach is a great ice breaker for both individual therapy and groups. I especially like to use this activity with kids who are not sure where to start with their sessions or who tend to say, "I don't know" in response to most questions.

Since most people have their photos organized by year, this activity works well for more general prompts as well. You can ask your client to share photographs of happy times, which lends itself to a discussion of positive feelings and experiences, though you could draw on other emotions as well. Here are some prompts I have used:

1. Show me a photo from a time when you were very happy.

2. Show me a photo of something that makes you smile.

3. Show me a photo of someone you love.

4. Show me a photo of something that is not around anymore, which you miss.

5. Show me a photo of something pretty.

6. Show me a photo from a time when you did something difficult.

7. Show me a photo of someone who helps you.

8.   Show me a photo from a trip or vacation.

9.   Show me a photo you took inside your house.

10. Show me a photo of some place you have not been but want to go.

Projective Cards

Suggested Age Group: 4 and up

Therapeutic Benefits: Creative expression, communication skills, exploration of emotions

Telehealth Benefits: A benefit of doing virtual card activities is that your cards will never get old or experience wear and tear because they are on the computer! You can also view each card simultaneously with your client rather than passing it back and forth.

Setup: If you own physical projective cards, you can hold them up to the camera. However, I find that clients have an easier time if I screen share images directly from my computer. Many images are available online, and Dr. Karen Fried has created several free projection cards on her website: https://www.oaklandertraining.org/projective -cards. You can either scroll through the options and have the client let you know when they see a card that reflects their mood today, or you can have the client pick a number (Dr. Fried's website has 55 cards to choose from) and pull up the card that coincides with that number.

Once you decide on a card, have your client tell a story about the image. Ask them to describe the character or characters in the story, including what the character is doing, thinking, and feeling. Reflect parts of the story back to them and note any themes that they bring up through this activity.

Story Cards

Suggested Age Group: 4 and up

Therapeutic Benefits: Creative expression, communication skills, exploration of emotions, exploration of relationships, attachment work

Telehealth Benefits: Virtual story cards never go missing, and if you want to make notes about the story for review later, it is easy to type in details while still making eye contact with your client through the camera.

Setup: If you have a physical card deck, you can do this activity by holding up each card to the camera. You can also use the virtual deck of cards provided here: https://deck .of.cards/. You can share your screen with your client—or you can click *multiplayer* and then *create multiplayer game*, and then send the link generated to your client. You will need to click *shuffle* a few times before starting, as the deck always starts off in the same order before shuffling.

Tell your client that you want to play a storytelling game. You will draw cards one at a time to tell a story, and you and your client will take turns adding to the story. (This activity can also work well in groups.) The object of the activity is to add to the story based on the cards you draw, but there is no set rule or guideline beyond this. For example, if you draw the four of hearts, you might talk about four people in a family who love each other. A queen, king, or jack might be a new character.

Note what comes up for your client in this activity, both in terms the story itself and their emotional response to the activity. Depending on your client's developmental level and the time available, choose how many cards you will use at the beginning. You can do a short story with only six cards (you and the client each have three turns) or have a much longer story. This activity can be done several times, and you will get a different story each time because the cards are drawn randomly.

What Would You Do?

Suggested Age Group: 8 and up

Therapeutic Benefits: Decision-making, social skills, understanding consequences, exploration of emotions

Telehealth Benefits: While it is easy enough to play What Would You Do? during in-person sessions, the telehealth format allows you to enhance this activity using video demonstrations and examples if desired. Simply pull up the video you want to use, share your screen (and sound), and watch the video together.

Setup: In this activity, you will be presenting your client with a series of hypothetical scenarios and asking how they would respond. If you are using a video to go along with this activity, cue it up and share your screen and audio with your client. The *What Would You Do?* television show has many great examples on their YouTube channel (https://www.youtube.com/c/WhatWouldYouDo/videos). However, you can also make up your own hypothetical situations based on your client's life experience or use some of the sample situations listed below:

1. You see a peer calling another peer names. What would you do? Does your answer change if the peer doing the name-calling is a friend of yours? What if the peer being called names was mean to you in the past?

2. You see a classmate copying answers from their neighbor on a test. What would you do? What if the classmate is your friend?

3. A peer who you don't like very much has been hanging out with your friend group. They aren't mean, but you find them annoying. What do you do?

4. What would you do if you found a wallet with money in it? What if there is no identification with the wallet?

5. You are having trouble with an assignment and ask your teacher for help. Your teacher says, "Come on, it isn't that hard" in a rough tone. What would you do?

Make sure that you query your client not to just say what they think the "right" answer is but to explore how they think they would actually respond in the situation. Then discuss whether they are happy with that choice or whether they wish they would do something different. Talk about how they can mindfully and deliberately change their responses to various situations.

Part **7**

Structured Skill-Building Activities

But wait, there's more! The activities in this section focus on different areas of mental health—including mindfulness, behavioral activation, and cognitive restructuring—through the use of structured skills-based interventions that do not involve play or games. Since these activities are not play-based, it can be helpful to implement them along with a more "fun" activity in the same session.

The 12 activities in this chapter will help drive home therapy skills, enhance cognitive behavioral techniques, and facilitate emotion processing. These activities are designed to help kids know how to practice skills such as deep breathing, mindful awareness, and self-regulation between sessions. They also emphasize addressing unsafe or problem behaviors from a cognitive behavioral standpoint to mitigate safety concerns. Although you can use many of these activities in an in-person setting, the setup and instructions are designed for use in telehealth sessions.

Ads for Mindfulness

Suggested Age Group: 6 and up

Therapeutic Benefits: Mindfulness, patience, emotion regulation, exploration of emotions, body work

Telehealth Benefits: Many telehealth games have advertisements, which is what the game creators use to cover the cost of webhosting. This can be annoying for therapists and clients alike because you have to wait for the ad to finish to start your game. However, this becomes an opportunity on its own to practice mindfulness skills, check in with emotions, and be patient.

Setup: Pull up whatever website you will be using for the session's telehealth activity and allow the advertisement to begin playing. The advertisement itself is not directly relevant to this intervention, so I recommend muting the game website. While the ad plays, cue your client to do some physical stretches or ask them a specific question while they wait. Suggested questions include:

1. What emotions are you experiencing right now, and where do you feel them in your body?

2. What is it like to have to wait?

3. When is another time you have had to be patient, and what happened?

4. What kinds of things are worth waiting for?

You can also present your client with a brief mindfulness script while you wait for the ad to finish playing. Feel free to come up with whatever script you feel is most appropriate, though you can also use the following sample script:

"Let's take a moment to breathe and check in with our bodies. Notice how your body is positioned right now. Is it comfortable? What muscles feel tense? Take a big breath in through your nose—1...2...3...4...5...—and out through your mouth—1...2...3...4...5...6...7. How did that breath change how your body feels? Where do you still feel tension? Take a moment to squeeze those tense muscles as tight as you can and then let that tension out."

Breath GIFs

Suggested Age Group: 4 and up

Therapeutic Benefits: Mindfulness, relaxation, body awareness

Telehealth Benefits: Breath GIFs make great tools for breath work because the client can see a visual representation of the activity. You can model how to practice deep breathing by sharing your screen and allowing the client to view you and the GIF at the same time.

Setup: Find the GIF you want to use and share your screen with your client. There are many breath GIFs available, some with continuous breathing and some with a pause between inhales and exhales. While you can search for GIFs on your own or with your client, here are links to some that I have found helpful:

- https://www.duffthepsych.com/wp-content/uploads/2016/07/478Breathe500 x500c129revised.gif

- https://media.self.com/photos/5979027b83c6610bb8c6be72/4:3/ w_2560%2Cc_limit/Deep-Breathing-Relax.gif

- https://media1.giphy.com/media/dDXZ3qU5nRBIe82Uit/giphy.gif

- https://media.giphy.com/media/l0HlBO95YqWIKaDRu/giphy.gif

- https://c.tenor.com/3FLoFGA4GowAAAAM/breathing-breathe.gif

Determine which style meets your client's needs. You can use the GIF to do a few centering breaths at the start or end of a session, or use it as an ongoing relaxation activity while talking through difficult topics. I have found it helpful with clients who are trying to share something emotional with me, and they breathe with the GIF as they tell me what is on their mind. You can use the breath GIF on its own or pair it with a specific mindfulness script.

Changing the Direction of the Train

Suggested Age Group: 6 and up

Therapeutic Benefits: Focus, cognitive restructuring, mindfulness

Telehealth Benefits: Many mindfulness activities require clients to practice mentally visualizing what is being described in the narration, but some clients struggle with visualization. GIF-based exercises are a great solution that provide clients with that visual component.

Setup: Because GIFs are made up of several photographs in succession, GIFs of moving trains that are on a loop ("never-ending" GIFs) can look like they are traveling either toward you or away from you. You can search "train GIF changing directions," "never-ending train GIF," or "train direction GIF" to find several options. The links below are examples I have used, though others are available:

1. **Single train:** https://i.imgur.com/TnfzrDD.gif?noredirect

2. **Two trains:** https://i.imgur.com/sYCsFEa.gif (with this image, you can challenge the client to imagine that each train is going a different way)

Once you decide on a GIF, share your screen with the client and use the following script to introduce the activity: "I am going to show you an image of a train. Tell me, is the train moving towards you or away from you? Okay, now I want you to focus on the train and see if you can make it move the other way. See how you can change the direction of the train simply by focusing on it? This is just like how you can change what direction your thoughts are going."

Then prompt your client to think of a time when their thoughts were going in an unhelpful direction. Have them imagine placing these thoughts on the train going in one direction. Explore what thoughts come up when they follow that train versus when they consciously push the train in the opposite direction.

Daily Behavior Goal

Suggested Age Group: 5 and up

Therapeutic Benefits: Behavior modification, decision-making, self-compassion

Telehealth Benefits: When you work with clients to set goals during in-person sessions, a lot of handwriting is involved. The telehealth platform allows you to type the client's ideas as they share them, making the activity flow more easily. Typed notes are also easier to review when you do not have to worry about deciphering handwriting.

Setup: Prior to the session, create a fillable PDF using the sample worksheet on the next page. I have used https://www.sejda.com/pdf-forms and https://www.jotform.com/fillable-pdf-form-creator/. These platforms are not HIPAA-complaint, so you should not upload any document with protected health information. However, they can be helpful in creating a worksheet template that you can use in therapy. You can save templates as a Word document or as a fillable PDF, depending on which works best for you.

At the start of the session, share your screen and let your client know that you want to create a behavior goal for them to try to reach each day. Have your client decide what kind of behavior they either want to do more or less of, and use the guiding questions on the worksheet to help them articulate a specific, attainable goal. You want to make sure their goal is specific enough that they can clearly tell when they have achieved it.

Explain that the great thing about a daily goal is, if they are not successful, they can always try again tomorrow. Every day is a new opportunity to succeed. At first, encourage your client to focus on reaching their goal just once per week; they can increase the frequency as they get better at reaching their goal. You can also have your client and their parent or guardian create a new goal each day or set a goal to work toward for several days in a row.

Daily Behavior Goal
Sample Worksheet

No matter what happened or what you did yesterday, today you are starting fresh. Today might not be perfect, but you have a new opportunity to try again!

What is your goal for today? What do you want to accomplish, and what would make today feel like a "good" day for you? How will you know if you are successful? What specifically would it look like if you reach this goal today?

_____

_____

_____

_____

What specific things do you need to do to make this goal a reality? You might list out things you tried in the past that did not work, things you want to try in the future, or support you need from the adults in your life to help you reach this goal.

1. _____

2. _____

3. _____

4. _____

5. _____

Daily Self-Care Checklist

Suggested Age Group: 5 and up

Therapeutic Benefits: Self-care, mindfulness, behavioral activation, communication skills

Telehealth Benefits: Telehealth simplifies the process of creating checklists in session, as you and your client can share screens and type the specific items on the client's checklist. Typed notes are easier to read than handwritten notes, and you can send a copy to your client or their parent/guardian while keeping an identical copy for your own notes and reference.

Setup: Before the session begins, create a fillable PDF using the sample worksheet on the next page. I have used https://www.sejda.com/pdf-forms and https://www.jotform.com/fillable-pdf-form-creator/ to create fillable PDFs for free. These platforms are not HIPAA-complaint, so you should not upload any document with protected health information. However, they can be helpful in creating a worksheet template that you can use in therapy. You can save templates as a Word document or as a fillable PDF, depending on which works best for you.

At the start of the session, share your screen with your client and use the following script to explain the activity: "There are different things we need to do every day to take care of our bodies and minds. We are going to list some things that you can do every day to be as healthy and feel as good as possible. I want you to use the list we come up with to take care of yourself every day. It is okay if you don't do every category every single day—this is just a starting point to help you."

This activity helps your client identify and communicate their self-care needs while also motivating them to follow through and meet those needs. The prompts allow them to identify any unmet meets and mindfully consider solutions that will work for them. It also helps them learn how to communicate their needs with you, which enhances their ability to talk about their needs with other adults outside of the therapy session.

Daily Self-Care
Sample Checklist

There are different things you can do every day to take care of your mind and body. Under each category below, list some things you can do to take care of yourself in that area. Remember, it is okay if you don't do each thing every single day, but you can try to do at least one activity from each category.

Keep my body healthy:

1. _____

2. _____

3. _____

Do a chore around the house:

1. _____

2. _____

3. _____

Do something kind for someone:

1. _____

2. _____

3. _____

Talk to someone:

1. _____

2. _____

3. _____

Learn one new thing:

1. _____

2. _____

3. _____

Do one creative thing:

1. _____

2. _____

3. _____

Move my body:

1. _____

2. _____

3. _____

Depression Nesting

Suggested Age Group: 10 and up

Therapeutic Benefits: Behavioral activation, self-compassion, self-care, exploration of emotions

Telehealth Benefits: Sometimes when someone is in the midst of a depressive episode, they "nest" in their room, accumulating dishes, food wrappers, and general messiness. As they come out of the episode, they might feel motivated to clean up their nest. However, this requires them to go through everything in the nest, which can be demoralizing and bring up negative self-talk about how they behaved while in the episode. The telehealth platform allows the therapist to join them in their depression "nest" and talk them through their emotions as they clean up, which promotes self-compassion and follow-through with the task.

Setup: This activity is appropriate after a client has emerged from a depressive episode. During the session, explain the concept of a depression "nest" and ask if this is something your client experienced during their episode. If the answer is yes, encourage them to have their session in their "nest" and to clean it up while you are present.

As your client goes through their space, ask them about their thoughts and emotional state. Reframe any negative self-talk about the nest and point out that the space helped them survive the depressive episode. If they become discouraged by the quantity of the mess, encourage them to keep going and clean up the space. Narrate their progress.

Depending on the client, the space, and the severity and length of the depressive episode, this may be too big of a job for a 45-minute or even a 60-minute session. Clients can also become overwhelmed by the size of the task. If they start the activity with an idea of what they want to do first, that's fine! But if they seem to be having trouble knowing where to start, have them scan the area with their camera. Point out a small, specific place (for example, "See that chair with all the laundry on it?" or "Let's start with the nightstand by your bed") and have them begin with a small and manageable chunk of the space. Guide them in doing one small section at a time.

If the session ends with more to do, let your client know that they can continue at their next appointment. However, use your clinical judgment here; if appropriate, you might have them continue going through the space in between appointments. If they express a lot of negative self-talk during the activity (for example, "I can't believe I let it get this bad" or "I'm such a slob, I'm so gross"), you might encourage them to wait until the next appointment before continuing with the task so you can address, process, and restructure these thoughts.

Exposure Therapy

Suggested Age Group: 14 and up

Therapeutic Benefits: Anxiety exposure, cognitive restructuring, exploration of emotions

Telehealth Benefits: Many cognitive behavioral therapists use in-vivo exposures in their in-person sessions. They might take the client to a setting that triggers anxiety and help them work through it in real time. If this involves leaving your office to a more public place, there are potential limits to confidentiality. The benefit of telehealth is that you can be on the phone with your client and talk them through the exposure in real time without being physically present and risking their privacy. Additionally, since you are not physically present, your client must engage in the exposure more independently than they would with an in-person exposure.

Setup: Plan for this activity prior to the session itself. Although the telehealth setting makes this activity more private than if you were physically present, you want to ensure that your client understands there are still possible confidentiality limitations of talking to you in a public place. Make sure that you get assent from your client, as well as appropriate consent from their guardian. Confirm that your client's chosen location for the session is physically safe and ask them to provide you with an address for safety purposes.

Then have your client join the session from your pre-chosen location. For clients with social anxiety, they might check in from a grocery store or a shop at the mall and go through the steps of making a purchase and potentially asking an employee for help. Process their emotions in real time using your preferred feelings scale.

Five Senses Grounding Technique

Suggested Age Group: 5 and up

Therapeutic Benefits: Mindfulness, coping skills, communication skills, exploration of emotions

Telehealth Benefits: This activity is a variation on a popular grounding technique where clients are prompted to identify what they can see, hear, feel, smell, and taste in the moment. When adapted for use in telehealth, you can prompt your client to find items in their home that stimulate each sense. This makes the activity more real and cues them to use coping skills and comfort items as needed outside of the session.

Setup: Begin by asking your client, "What do you know about your five senses?" and allow them to explain what they know. Correct any information as needed and explain any senses they struggle to articulate. Then continue with the following script: "There are things in your home that you can see, hear, feel, smell, and taste. I want you to show me things that give you good feelings for each of your senses." You can then use the following prompts to help your client pick items for each sense. Make sure to have permission from the guardian to get these items, especially any food your client wants to incorporate.

1. Show me something that you like to look at, something that makes your eyes happy. What do you like about this thing? What makes it fun to look at?

2. Show me something that makes a sound you like. How does it feel to hear that sound?

3. What is something that you like to touch? What does it feel like? What emotions does that texture bring up for you?

4. What is something in your house that smells really good to you? What does it smell like? What does that smell remind you of?

5. What is something in your house that tastes really good to you? Take a small bite right now and chew it very slowly. Try to really taste all the different flavors. What was that like for you?

Press Pause on Impulsivity

Suggested Age Group: 6 and up

Therapeutic Benefits: Impulse control, decision-making, understanding consequences, behavior modification, mindfulness, guided visualization

Telehealth Benefits: With telehealth, you can literally have kids practice pausing a video as a way to visualize what it's like to "press pause" on an unwanted behavior in real life. To make the activity more engaging, you can use a video from your client's favorite content creator or a show that they enjoy. Have them demonstrate "pressing pause" in real time during the video, identifying moments when the character could stop and think about their behavior.

Setup: Decide with your client what piece of media you will use for this activity. Ideally, choose a clip that involves a character or individual making an unfortunate choice or doing something they are not supposed to do. It can help to choose the video (and the corresponding scene) in your previous session so you are prepared and have the right scene cued up at the start of the session.

Pull up the video (you can use YouTube or a streaming service such as Netflix or Hulu), share your screen, and grant your client remote control. Start the video and have your client literally press pause on the video at relevant "stop and think" moments. While the video is paused, discuss what choices the character has and the possible consequences of those choices.

As your client gets better at recognizing the connection between actions and consequences using the video scenarios, you can have them apply this activity to their own life. Ask your client to think about a recent time when they made a choice that they later regretted. Ask them what they did and what they wished they had done differently. Then use the script below (or an appropriate variation) to help them learn the skill of stopping to think before engaging in a behavior:

"Imagine that you are watching yourself on a screen. You see yourself going about your day, making choices and doing different things. Now look down at your hand, and imagine you are holding a remote control. Look back at the screen and see yourself right before you _____ [behavior or choice they regretted] _____. Find the pause button on your remote, and press it. This causes you to freeze on the screen! Now that you are paused, you can think through different options about how you might react instead. What might you be able to do differently? What other choices could you make, and what would the outcomes of those choices be?"

Explore different alternatives and tell your client that the next time they are in a similar situation, they could pause and think about choices before acting. To expand on this activity, you can go on to further explore choices:

"Maybe sometimes you do not hit the pause button fast enough, and you've already made a choice. That is okay! You can still rewind after the fact and see what might have caused you to make a choice so quickly. You can notice what things led up to that choice so you can look out for them in the future. And you can always press pause after the choice as a way to apologize and fix your mistakes.

"Adults can also help you remember to press pause. But you don't have to wait for them to remind you! You can press pause any time you want to think before making a choice. You can let the adults around you know that you are pressing pause so they can patiently wait for you to make a choice or help you figure out what your options are."

Who Would Win?

Suggested Age Group: 7 and up

Therapeutic Benefits: Critical thinking, decision-making, problem-solving, communication skills

Telehealth Benefits: Character battle mashups are incredibly popular on sites such as Reddit. You can see different people's opinions about the outcome, as well as their rationale to challenge your client's conclusions.

Setup: This activity is particularly fun with clients who enjoy movies, shows, or other media with a lot of action or fighting. Have them talk about their preferred franchise and the characters in it. When they're done sharing, ask them to choose two characters and to imagine that these characters are fighting each other. Ask who they think would win the fight and why. They can choose characters from the same universe ("Who would win if the Joker fought Two Face?") or mix and match ("Who would win if Mewtwo fought Godzilla?"). Some good franchises for this activity are:

1. Marvel Universe

2. DC Universe

3. Godzilla and the MonsterVerse

4. Power Rangers

5. Pokémon

6. Star Wars

7. Five Nights at Freddy's

You and your client can write down your guesses, and then share to see if you came to the same conclusion. Take turns sharing your reasoning. If you did not agree, take turns sharing why you each came to your conclusion and practice disagreeing respectfully.

Part 8

8

Games by Device

One challenge of telehealth is that the options available to you can vary depending on the platform you are using, the type of device you and your client are on, and the quality of the client's internet connection. It can be difficult to quickly determine which activities are available to you based on these different factors, so I have broken it down for you here. In this section, you'll find a directory of all activities described in this book, as well as in the first volume of *Telemental Health*, categorized by tech option available to you. Simply go to the section that fits your available resources for a given session.

Within this directory, I've included references to volume number and page number so you easily find each activity. Between Volume I and Volume II of *Telemental Health with Kids Toolbox*, this directory provides you with more than 225 kid-friendly telehealth interventions to choose from. My hope is that this gives you plenty of options for all clients, regardless of what device they are using, the quality of their internet connection, their areas of interest, and the platform you are using for your sessions. Hopefully this means you do not have to worry about running out of fresh, new ideas for a long, long time.

Link Share

If both you and your client have stable internet connection, and the client is able to access game websites, these activities involve sharing a link or password to a private room in which you and your client can play a game together. These activities might not be accessible if the client is meeting with you from school and the school's wireless connection blocks non-academic websites.

Name of Game	Vol/Pg #
Battleship	1/11
Carrom	2/7
Cars	1/113
Chess	1/14
Connect Four	1/16
Crazy Eights	1/17
Darts	2/10
Deck of Cards	1/98
Dominoes	1/18
Go Fish	1/22
Grabble	1/24
Guess Who	1/25
Hide-and-Seek	1/118
Jigsaw Puzzles	1/27
Mancala	1/29
Mastermind	2/82
Match Up	1/30
Minecraft	1/121
Narwhale	2/25
Pictionary	1/31
Scattergories	1/33
Speed	2/38
Story Cards	2/148
Tic Tac Toe	1/35
Uno	1/38

Screen Share with Remote Control

If the client is unable to access a specific link, the activities in this section allow you and the client to play together when you pull up the website on your end, share your screen, and grant the client remote control. They involve either taking turns with remote control or letting the client control your screen.

Name of Game	Vol/Pg #
Auto Draw	1/42
Beautiful Mind Games	2/72
Bomb Defuse	2/74
Bop It	2/122
Bottle Flip	2/75
Bowling	2/5
Character Creator	2/95
Checkers	1/13
Chess	1/14
Choose Your Own Adventure	2/97
Color by Numbers	2/100
Coloring Book	2/101
Comic Strips	2/103
Coping Skills Toolbox	1/134
Dadish	2/76
Diamond Art	2/106
Dollhouse	1/114
Dream Home Design	2/107
Dress-Up	2/123
Ducklings	2/124
Escape Rooms	1/116
Extreme Thumb War	2/12
Fidgets	1/75
Find in Mind	2/77
Find It/Hidden Objects	2/78
Fireworks	1/76

Get Over It	2/127
Glowit	2/17
Good Vibes	2/128
Hatchimals	1/117
Hexa Parking	2/79
Hexxagon	1/26
Hole	2/80
Jigsaw Puzzles	1/27
LEGO®	1/119
Lite Brite	2/109
Ludo	1/28
Magnet Poetry	2/110
Making Squares	2/21
Marble Run	2/111
Match Up	1/30
Mazes	1/120
Othello	2/26
Parcheesi	2/27
Penguin Wars	2/28
Pick Up Sticks	2/84
Polybusiness	2/30
Pool (8 Ball Billiards Classic)	2/32
Pop-It	2/33
Puppet Show	1/123
Role-Plays	2/131
Sand Drawing	1/54
Sand Painting	1/55
Sand Tray: Free Play	1/87
Sandscapes	1/56
Simon	2/87
Slime	1/89
Snakes and Ladders	1/34
Thought-Stopping Activity: Skip the Song	1/140
Tornado Brain	1/141

Trivia	1/36
Tumbling Tower	1/37
Tunnel	2/89
Vision Boards	1/107
Vision Boards: Challenges	2/115
Vision Boards: Life Goals	2/117
Vision Boards: What Makes Me Happy	2/118
Vision Boards: Who Loves Me	2/119
Weave Silk	1/58
Wonderfully Juicy	2/91
Yahtzee	1/40
Zen Photon Garden	1/92
Zen Rock Garden	1/91
Zilch	2/49

Screen Share with Remote Keyboard Control

As with the last section, these activities involve sharing your screen and granting the client remote control to engage in the activity. However, they require that the client have access to a keyboard. Therefore, they work well with laptops but might not be an available option if the client is on a smartphone or tablet.

Name of Game	Vol/Pg #
2048	2/52
Animals Minigame Party	2/2
Bad Ice Cream	2/53
Badminton	2/3
Basket Random	2/4
Boxing Random	2/6
City Car Stunt	2/8
Cuphead	2/54
Dance Party II	2/9
Dino Squad Adventure	2/55
DinoZ City	2/56
Donut vs Donut	2/11
Duo Survival	1/19
Etch A Sketch	1/49
Extreme Speedboat Driving	2/125
Fire of Belief	2/58
Fireboy and Watergirl	2/57
Fish Eat Fishes	2/13
Food Duel	2/14
Foosball	1/21
Foosball 3D	2/15
Get On Top	2/16
Gun Mayhem	2/19
Gun Mayhem Co-Op	2/59

Interplanetary	2/60
Ironic Zombie	2/61
Last Survivors	2/62
Lost Pyramid	2/63
Meteor Shower	2/23
Mike & Munk	2/64
Minecraft	1/121
Miners' Adventure	2/65
Mini Heads Party	2/24
Money Movers	2/66
Pizza Challenge	2/29
Plot Generator	2/112
Pong	2/31
Rock, Paper, Scissors	2/34
Rooftop Snipers	2/35
Snowball Skirmish	2/36
Soccer Random	2/37
Space Prison Escape	2/67
Speed Boat Extreme Racing	2/39
Sprinter Heroes	2/40
Tag	1/127
Tube Jumpers	2/42
Tug the Table	2/44
Tug-of-War	2/43
Tunnel Rush	2/45
Two Ball 3D	2/46
Unfair Mario	2/90
Volley Random	2/47
Wrestle Jumping	2/48
Zombie Mission X	2/68
Zoom-Be	2/69

Screen Share (Client)

These activities involve the client sharing their screen with you. This can be great for relationship building because the client can show you something they have created or a game they enjoy on their end. Many of these activities have the option for you to join the client in the platform, but if you don't want to worry about your own skills with a particular platform, you can also observe the client, narrate play, and talk through things while they show you their world.

Name of Game	Vol/Pg #
Antistress Game	1/74
Auto Draw	1/42
Beautiful Mind Games	2/72
Bomb Defuse	2/74
Bop It	2/122
Bottle Flip	2/75
Bowling	2/5
Character Creator	2/95
Checkers	1/13
Chess	1/14
Color by Numbers	2/100
Coloring Book	2/101
Comic Strips	2/103
Coping Skills Toolbox	1/134
Dadish	2/76
Diamond Art	2/106
Dollhouse	1/114
Dream Home Design	2/107
Dress-Up	2/123
Ducklings	2/124
Duo Survival	1/19
Escape Rooms	1/116
Etch A Sketch	1/49
Extreme Thumb War	2/12

Fidgets	1/75
Find in Mind	2/77
Find It/Hidden Objects	2/78
Fireworks	1/76
Foosball	1/21
Get Over It	2/127
Glowit	2/17
Good Vibes	2/128
Hatchimals	1/117
Hexa Parking	2/79
Hexxagon	1/26
Hole	2/80
Jigsaw Puzzles	1/27
LEGO®	1/119
Lite Brite	2/109
Ludo	1/28
Magnet Poetry	2/110
Marble Run	2/111
Match Up	1/30
Minecraft	1/121
Othello	2/26
Parcheesi	2/27
Penguin Wars	2/28
Photo Share	2/145
Pick Up Sticks	2/84
Plot Generator	2/112
Polybusiness	2/30
Pool (8 Ball)	2/32
Pop-It	2/33
Puppet Show	1/123
Roblox: Adopt Me	1/124
Roblox: Hide-and-Seek	1/125
Roblox: Meep City	1/126
Roblox Potion Experiments (Wacky Wizards)	2/86

Role-Plays   2/131
Sand Drawing   1/54
Sand Painting   1/55
Sand Tray: Free Play   1/87
Sandscapes   1/56
Simon   2/87
Slime   1/89
Snakes and Ladders   1/34
Thought-Stopping Activity: Stop the Song   1/140
Tornado Brain   1/141
Trivia   1/36
Tumbling Tower   1/37
Tunnel   2/89
Unfair Mario   2/90
Vision Boards   1/107
Vision Boards: Challenges   2/115
Vision Boards: Life Goals   2/117
Vision Boards: What Makes Me Happy?   2/118
Vision Boards: Who Loves Me?   2/119
Weave Silk   1/58
Wonderfully Juicy   2/91
Yahtzee   1/40
Zen Photon Garden   1/92
Zen Rock Garden   1/91

Screen Share
without Remote Control

This section details activities that will work when you can share your screen but your client is on a device that does not allow remote control. This can complicate certain games because the client cannot freely manipulate the activity themselves. However, this can be a way to promote communication skills and behavior rehearsal, as they have to direct you in the activity.

Name of Game	Vol/Pg #
Body Stretches	1/61
Breath GIFs	2/153
Changing the Direction of the Train	2/154
Charades	1/62
Checkers	1/13
Chess	1/14
Choose Your Own Adventure	2/97
Daily Behavior Goal	2/155
Daily Self-Care Checklist	2/157
Dance Party	1/63
Deck of Cards	1/98
Hexxagon	1/26
I Can Make My Heart Go Fast	1/65
Ludo	1/28
Mad Libs	2/140
Mirroring	1/66
Muscle Relaxation	1/67
My Needs	2/141
Nature Cams	2/129
Paper Airplanes	2/130
Parcheesi	2/27
Perception: What Color Do You See?	1/85
Pet Finder	2/144

Polybusiness   2/30
Projective Cards   2/147
Reaction Videos and Emotion Identification   1/135
Role-Plays   2/131
Roller Coaster VR   2/133
Scavenger Hunt   1/68
Shake Out the Wiggles   1/69
Simon Says   1/70
Snakes and Ladders   1/34
Story Cards   2/148
Tornado Brain   1/141
Trivia   1/36
Virtual Vacations   1/106
Wake Up Your Face Muscles!   1/71
Wish List   2/135
Yahtzee   1/40
Zilch   2/49

No Tech Available

Sometimes you might not be able to share a link or share your screen. These activities can be done if no website or tech options are available, which may occur if you are in an office that blocks game websites, or the client is at school and unable to access these websites. These activities will also work if you are both using Chrome books, which do not allow for screen control. Because you cannot rely on the tech, some of these activities involve having items on hand, such as printer paper, but for accessibility reasons, I tried to keep additional supplies to a minimum.

Name of Game	Vol/Pg #
Alphabet Game	1/94
Auto Complete Game	1/96
Battleship (each on your own Battleship board game)	1/11
Big Breath Activities	1/132
Body Stretches	1/61
Camping Trip Drawing: Joint Drawing Task (with physical paper)	1/43
Charades	1/62
Chat: Secrets	2/138
Chats	1/97
Chess (set up chess in your office as the client instructs you)	1/14
Creating a Sensory Space	2/104
Dance Party	1/63
Deck of Cards (with a physical deck of cards)	1/98
Depression Nesting	2/160
Draw a Garden: Joint Drawing Task (with physical paper)	1/44
Draw Your Family (with physical paper)	1/45
Draw Your Feelings (with physical paper)	1/46
Draw Your Home (with physical paper)	1/48
Emoji Reactions	2/139
Exposure Therapy	2/162
Fear Drawing (with physical paper)	1/50
Filters	2/126
Five Senses Grounding Technique	2/163

Guess Who? (each on your own Guess Who? board game)   1/25
I Can Make My Heart Go Fast   1/65
Mandala Drawing (with physical paper)   1/51
Meet Your Pets   1/101
Mindful Hearing   1/77
Mindful Seeing   1/79
Mindful Smelling   1/81
Mindful Tasting   1/83
Mindful Touch   1/84
Mirroring   1/66
Muscle Relaxation   1/67
Origami/Paper Folding   1/52
Physical Play   1/122
Pictionary (with physical paper)   1/31
Press Pause on Impulsivity   2/164
Receiving Help   1/136
Riddles   2/85
Safe Place Drawing (with physical paper)   1/53
Safety Planning   1/137
Scavenger Hunt   1/68
Self-Portrait Drawing (with physical paper)   1/57
Sentence Stories   1/102
Shake Out the Wiggles   1/69
Simon Says   1/70
Snowman (with physical paper)   2/88
Story Cards (with physical cards)   2/148
Thought Record   1/139
Three Songs   1/103
Tic Tac Toe (with physical paper as the client instructs you) 1/35
Timeline   2/113
Trivia   1/36
Twenty Questions   1/104
Virtual Backgrounds   1/128
Wake Up Your Face Muscles!   1/71

What If You Were a _____?   1/59

What Would You Do?   2/149

Who Would Win?   2/166

Wish List   2/135

Would You Rather   1/108

Yahtzee (with physical dice)   1/40

Your Story   1/110

Zilch (with physical dice)   2/49

Whiteboards

Finally, here you will find activities that can be done using the whiteboard feature available on many telehealth platforms. If the platform you are using does not include a whiteboard feature, you can use Whiteboard Fox with a private room or screen share with Microsoft Paint for most of these activities.

Name of Game	Vol/Pg #
Auto Complete Game	1/96
Buddha Board	2/94
Camping Trip Drawing: Joint Drawing Task	1/43
Coloring Book	2/101
Draw a Garden: Joint Drawing Task	1/44
Draw Your Family	1/45
Draw Your Feelings	1/46
Draw Your Home	1/48
Fear Drawing	1/50
Making Squares	2/21
Mandala Drawing	1/51
Mazes	1/120
Safe Place Drawing	1/53
Self-Portrait Drawing	1/57
Snowman	2/88
Vision Boards	1/107
What If You Were a _____?	1/59